ALONE, BUT NOT LONELY:

Aging On Your Terms

A Roadmap for Aging Independently, Striking Balance & Finding Purpose

CHRÍO ZOË

CONTENTS

ACKNOWLEDGEMENT

Writing this book has been a labor and a journey that I couldn't have undertaken without the incredible support and encouragement of many individuals. I am profoundly grateful to all those who have played a part in bringing this project to fruition.

I would like to thank each person who was instrumental in shaping my path to writing this manuscript. My sincerest appreciation goes to the countless friends and family who graciously gave me space and time to make this book become a reality.

First and foremost, I want to express my deepest gratitude to my family whose unwavering belief in me and constant encouragement have been my driving force. Your love and support have sustained me through the challenges of this creative process. I give honor to my late parents, whose unwavering belief has been the catalyst to propel me in this journey. Their constant encouragement and unconditional love have been my strength to pursue this endeavor. I say thank you to my siblings Michael, Anthony, Pauline and Sharon who have now passed on but are the silent voices that ignited me to write this book. Through their life, in their own small contributing way, I have come to realize that this journey we call life is valuable and how we start the journey does not dictate how we finish it.

I would like to thank all of my mentors and teachers who helped me by sharing their invaluable knowledge base with me, as they guided me from a place of knowing in shaping my ideas and refining my writing. I cherish your warm guidance, encouragement, and belief in me, and my potential and I can attest to the fact that it has been transformative. I am sincerely hoping that this book will serve as a helpful resource and companion guide on my readers' journey toward self-improvement, empowerment, and fulfillment.

I'd also like to thank the team at AIA and Publishing Services for their dedication and hard work in bringing this book to life. Your expertise coaching and guidance in outlining, design, formatting, and marketing have been pivotal in turning my manuscript into a polished publication.

Additionally, I am grateful to my dear friends, who provided much-needed moral support and encouragement during the writing process. I am forever grateful for your influence and for your push to encourage me into what you believe I could be. Thank you all for the guidance and the wisdom you shared with me as I stumbled along my sometimes-rocky road of personal growth and self-discovery. I extend my heartfelt appreciation to my friends and colleagues who provided valuable feedback, engaged in insightful discussions, and cheered me on during moments of doubt. Your enthusiasm has been contagious and uplifting.

Finally, I want to acknowledge my readers—those who will engage with this book. Your curiosity and interest in my ideas fuel my passion for writing, and I hope this book resonates with you in meaningful ways. In writing this book, I've come to realize that the journey is made sweeter by the presence of supportive souls. To all those I've mentioned and to anyone whose name might have been inadvertently omitted, please know that your impact has been immeasurable.

To all of you, your enthusiasm, engagement, and support to me have been more than appreciated. Let me end by saying once again to my readers that I applaud you for buying this book to enhance and empower your personal development. I trust that this book will meet your desire.

With heartfelt thanks,

Chrío Zoë

INTRODUCTION

One of the big fears that people have about aging is that elderly people are lonely and boring people. I will tell you now that I used to have the same thoughts too, until I began to observe my father in his later years. He was 70 years old at the time, and lonely and boring were not among his problems. From time to time, I would watch my father in our front yard, making merry with his old friends and the new friends he met at the community center. Their gatherings were always an enriching experience distinguished by enthusiastic social bonding and joyfulness. This was when I realized that aging does not automatically mean living a boring and lonely life; it is the decisions you make as you grow older that count.

That said, it is not unusual to see aging and older people experience a feeling of isolation, or to find themselves, for different reasons, with no friends and no social groups they can identify with, increasing their risk of loneliness. Sometimes, anxieties, mental health, and different number of age-related challenges can make it more difficult for older people to socialize and build social connections. However, the lack of a thriving social life can worsen the state of mind of aging and older adults, and it can also shorten lifespan in the case of serious depression, negative self-talk, and a pessimistic view of life. People in general feel more alive and useful when they know they have a community of people that will always have their back and encourage them throughout their journey in life. This is especially true for older adults whose mobility and physical strength may no longer be the same as during their youth. However, one of the things you will learn in this book is that loneliness is not an exclusive problem of older people only. The popular opinion that as you grow older, you become lonelier is a myth and overestimated misrepresentation.

At the same time, social isolation, loneliness, and lack of social groups can be really harmful to older people in the long term. This is partly because the people who fall into that age bracket grew up in communities and social circles that may not be as strong or in existence now. Unlike the younger people in this generation, older adults appreciate strong communal bonding and do not do well when they have to do life alone. Without a sense of belonging, life can quickly become tedious and sad, especially for older people. At the end of the day, the quality of the social life of seniors can have a significant impact on their health, lifespan, and their overall view of life. In fact, a crucial study has shown that "308,000 participants found that participants with strong social connections had a 50 percent increased likelihood of survival across age, sex, and initial health status" (McMullen, 2021). I know this to be true. I know that those community events and social gatherings helped my father to be happier and more positive in his view about life. In hindsight, it is clear to me that my father identified the best way to age on his own terms and chose to never look back. For most older people, getting old is a process that reveals life in old age is significantly different from life in your earlier years.

Life happens, and things that you may have enjoyed fully in your earlier years like a close-knit family, a strong support system, and a happy team of lovely friends may not be the same in your old age. Your children might outgrow your family home and neighborhood, and your friends might move to different neighborhoods, pass away, or be distracted by many other things in life. As a result, you may quickly realize that you are alone and not as socially connected as you used to be. Unlike before, the chances that you will have someone to hang out with, or someone to care for you when you are ill might quickly become really low. But you need to know that these developments are common with older adults, and they are hints that you may have to strengthen your past connections or build a new system of social and psychological support. This is perfectly normal and, like my father, there are many different things you can do to improve the quality of your life, whether it is the big things or the small things. In the same way, you can trust that this book will teach you how to build lasting social connections that will help you live a more beautiful and happy life in your older years.

In this book, we will look at the root causes of loneliness and isolation among aging and older adults. We will also look at the factors that can worsen or improve these problems, including the role of friendships, sense of purpose, lifestyle, and social connections. Equally, you will learn how to constantly assess your lifestyle and relationships in relation to certain clues and practices that can help improve the quality of your life. Also, you will learn about the difference between loneliness and being alone, and how you can use that knowledge to your advantage as you grow older. You will also learn how to open yourself up to new opportunities without losing yourself or feeling too vulnerable in the process. My goal is to show you that with good planning and a better social life anything is possible, even for older adults and seniors. The results of sticking to the things you learn in this book will help you find genuine and eternal happiness, fulfilment, and usefulness.

Through carefully curated expert information on how to make quality decisions to ward off isolation, loneliness, and other age-related issues that can shorten your lifespan, this book will give you a sense of renewed hope about the aging process. As long as you keep an open mind, this book will show you how healthy relationships play a vital role in living a healthy and long life, as well as the tips you can always practice to keep your healthy relationships alive. My hope is that, at the end of the book, aging and older adults would feel more confident about their decisions to improve their social life and, in the process, improve their mental and physical health as well.

CHAPTER 1

BEING ALONE VS. FEELING LONELY

There is a chance that you may experience being alone and loneliness in your old age, but that does not mean the two are the same. While being alone is not exactly a bad thing, if it is not done within a reasonable boundary, it can quickly result in and worsen loneliness. According to Norman Cousins, "the eternal quest of the human being is to shatter his loneliness." This is true because loneliness can lead to depression and cause serious mental, physical, and overall harm to your health. But if you do not properly define the boundaries between loneliness and solitude, you will likely encounter many frustrations in your attempt to escape loneliness. This is because you need to be alone and enjoy your solitude from time to time. If you enjoy your solitude enough, you will find that the other things you do to escape loneliness will complement your life better and make you happier.

THE DIFFERENCE BETWEEN ALONE AND LONELY

To be able to properly separate loneliness from solitude, you have to correctly understand the two and how to manage both situations the right way. Basically, loneliness is a feeling or emotional response that comes from knowing you are going through life alone, which can be a lot in your old age and as you grow older. Loneliness can come in different ways to different people. If you are someone who has always had people around you growing up, you will find it difficult to cope when you suddenly have to be alone for a lot of time. People who have always had a thriving social circle do better and live happier when that circle is always available to them. Sometimes it is the changes in your personal life or the changes in the life of friends that cause you to suddenly realize how lonely you actually are. There are also times when loneliness comes from feeling frustrated with things that may be going on in your life. It could be the result of a divorce, your children or grandchildren moving on to other things in their own life, or relocating to a new country or continent far away from what you have always known, or an unexpected change in general that affects the quality of your social life and human support system. When things like this happen to people, it is very likely that they will begin to feel lonely, sooner or later, and this can affect their general health and likelihood of living a long life.

Equally, it is possible to feel lonely when the quality of your social life is below the quantity that you perceive to be appropriate for you. You might be married and still feel like something is missing in your life, and your partner is not helping you locate that thing or improve your state of mind. In the same way, you might keep a group of friends around you and still feel like you are hanging out with the wrong crowd and somehow don't know how to live a more fulfiling life. So, the lack of a friendly community and the lack of genuine social connections can cause you to feel lonely a lot. The first tip to avoiding this pothole is to make sure you are associating with people who share the same interests as you do. In this regard, Killam (2020) has observed that

> 47 percent of people surveyed in a national study reported that their relationships are not meaningful, 58 percent said that no one knows them well, and 61 percent felt like their interests were not shared by the people around them. That's why it's not the number of social ties you have, but the quality of those social ties that matters most.

The right associations will speed up the process of forming genuine connections that can help you avoid loneliness and the lonely life. These connections can help you get through the difficult times in life, as well as the good times when all you want to do is joke around and have a lot of fun. Don't forget that having plenty of fun moments is an important ingredient for older adults and longevity in general. Also, it is important to acknowledge the fact that avoiding loneliness is not the same thing as never being alone, which brings us to the other side of this equation. The state of being alone or solitude is a significant part of our lives as humans. It is about spending time with yourself, connecting with your inner voice, discovering new things, and understanding old things in new ways.

Solitude is not a bad thing. In fact, it is very good for people in general and older adults in particular. It helps to enhance reflection and can also boost your sense of purpose and usefulness. The time you spend with yourself should be sacred and cherished, because it will help you enjoy and appreciate solitude more. For people who are natural introverts, they like to see solitude as a blessing. But this is also true for many people who are extroverts. Spending time alone with yourself is how you learn to recharge and blend your energy and soul into one positive force for your own peace, happiness, and enjoyment. In the same way, spending more time with yourself can help you deal with loneliness better.

Everyone feels lonely once in a while, and sometimes the best way to deal with loneliness is to enjoy being with yourself. In fact, there are times when you will have no other choice than to be by yourself. For example, during the period of the COVID-19 pandemic, Zaraska (2023) shows that roughly 36% of Americans complained about "serious loneliness." There is a good chance that these people might have coped better if they knew the tips for enjoying solitude during hard times. So, the more time you spend enjoying your solitude, the more likely it is that you will be able to deal with your loneliness better.

At the same time, there are many different things you can practice to help you enjoy your solitude better. We will look more into these tips as we proceed. For now, keep in mind that it is not enough to want to build connections with other people; it is crucial that you actually learn to connect with yourself, too. In fact, some will argue that the most important connection you can make is the connection you make with yourself. However, you will want to make sure that you do not let your love of solitude overwhelm the need for social connections with other people. This can easily lead to loneliness and depression. It is harder to fight your way out of that horrific state of mind than it is to build genuine connections with other people. It has been said that "If you get stuck in negative thinking or judgment around your loneliness, it can impact your desire to interact with others and make it harder to feel comfortable and confident socially" (Garis, 2020). So you will want to make sure you balance out the quality time you spend alone and the connections you form with other people. The axiom that humans are social creatures is true for everyone, especially older adults.

The Psychology of Loneliness

Psychology experts agree that there is indeed something known as the psychology of loneliness. In general, people are familiar with being lonely, but not everyone knows why they get lonely. To a large extent, loneliness is becoming an epidemic all around the world across different age groups. In a crucial study, it was revealed that "As many as 80% of individuals under the age of 18 and 40% of those over the age of 65 report being lonely" (Madeson, 2023). In fact, one other study revealed that "22% of Americans and 23% of British people said they felt lonely always or often" (Karaska, 2023). Additionally, another study reported that "nearly half of adults in the US experience feelings of loneliness daily" (Madeson, 2023). This is why the psychology of loneliness is important, because it helps to bridge the gap between being lonely and understanding the reason why and dealing with it appropriately. According to Kharicha (2019),

> We know a lot about the factors that can lead to older people feeling isolated and excluded and the life events that can contribute or trigger loneliness in later life. But we know less about the 'internal' factors that can shape someone's experience of loneliness and cause loneliness to become more severe.

The reason why this observation is crucial is that it helps us question the reason why many older people experience loneliness. In addition, Kharicha (2019) believes that "How people understand why they are lonely can also make a difference to their experience of loneliness. Loneliness can become chronic if it is seen as something we cannot change." This is basically what the psychology of loneliness is about. It is about discovering the inner voices that make loneliness seem like a weight that cannot be lifted when you get old. Contrary to the negativity of those voices, if you think about loneliness a little differently, it can be very advantageous. For example, you can think of loneliness as a phase that reminds you of what you are lacking in social connections and meaningful relationships.

This is significant because, if the experts are right that how we think about loneliness can help us deal with loneliness better, then there is no harm in seeing loneliness as another reason why you should invest in social connectedness. In fact, it has been observed that "Just as hunger motivates us to look for food, loneliness should drive us to seek out connection to others" (Karaska, 2023). Additionally, it has been observed that it helps to "think of loneliness as an invitation to check in with ourselves, reflect on our social health needs, and take action to prioritize connection. Loneliness can also be a source of creativity, inspiring artists and writers to express their experiences" (Killam, 2020).

Also, always remember there are some myths that cause confusion about loneliness and social isolation and can make it more difficult for you to grow out of loneliness and improve your social cr other coonnection skills. According to Killam (2020), "social isolation is the objective state of being alone. In contrast, loneliness is the subjective experience of disconnection. This means that you could be around other people, yet still feel lonely." Similarly, Subramanian (2020) has defined social isolation "the lack of contact with people in a social environment," adding that the "Potential warning signs include living alone, having few social ties, and minimal social contact." For Subramanian (2020), "Social isolation is as bad for your health as smoking a half a pack of cigarettes a day or of being obese, especially in the elderly." In fact, a relevant study has shown that "the increased likelihood of death was 26 percent for people who reported being lonely, 29 percent for those who were socially isolated, and 32 percent for those living alone" (Subramanian, 2020). In the same way, it is believed that "Veterans are particularly at risk for social isolation and loneliness, which can increase the risk of depression, anxiety, substance abuse, and suicide" (Subramanian, 2020). Knowing the difference between loneliness and social isolation can help you better understand how to react in both situations.

Another myth about loneliness is that it is easy to detect by doctors. Experts believe is the more often not true, and the reason it can be difficult to detect is that people who suffer from serious loneliness, particularly men, hardly go to the doctor, and when they do, they do not speak about the way they are feeling. According to Subramanian (2020), the common signs of extreme social isolation and loneliness that individuals, older people, and professionals can look out for are "drooling, tremor, a mask-like face, slow movement, an unpredictable bladder, poor fine motor skills, trouble walking, and slurred speech or a soft voice; as well as a real risk of falling." In the same way, while loneliness is popularly associated with getting old by aging and older adults, various studies have shown that it is a problem with high prevalence among the young and the "very old." In about 40 different surveys, it was found that "loneliness is common only among the very old. Between 20 and 30% (depending on the cross-sectional survey) of middle-aged and young-old respondents report moderate or serious loneliness" (Dykstra, 2009). The surveys also showed that "at advanced ages, the prevalence of loneliness increases. Of those aged 80 and over, 40–50% say they are "often" lonely" (Dykstra, 2009). However, they equally showed that "the prevalence of loneliness is also high among the youngest respondents, those between the ages of 15 and 24" (Dykstra, 2009). As a result, the overestimation of loneliness being a problem of old people in general is a myth. According to Dykstra (2009),

> The extent of loneliness among older people was overestimated in scope by the elderly themselves, although generally not to the degree of overestimation among Americans under the age of 65. Sixty-one percent of 18–34-year olds, 47% of 35–64-year olds, and 33% of

those aged 65 and above perceived loneliness as a serious problem "for most people over 65". Thirteen percent of those aged 65 and over gave an affirmative answer to the question of whether loneliness was "a serious problem … for [them] personally". In other words, people tend to attribute higher levels of loneliness to the elderly than the elderly themselves experience.

That said, you will want to keep in mind that the disadvantages of loneliness are too many to ignore. Loneliness can practically magnify sadness and depression and significantly reduce your self-esteem and sense of self. Additionally, loneliness can derail your sense of purpose and further reduce your ability to age with grace and make more positive impact in life. Also, loneliness "causes people to feel empty, alone, and unwanted. People who are lonely often crave human contact, but their state of mind makes it more difficult to form connections with others. (Madeson, 2023)." This state of mind can also affect your ability to connect with other people without feeling like they will eventually betray you or leave you just like everyone before them.

In this regard, loneliness can make you feel like you are not good enough and constantly make you feel like there is no reason to be alive. It can also make negative past experiences appear bigger than they actually are, causing you to be more unwilling to tackle the root of your loneliness. In fact, research has proven that loneliness can "decreases cognitive performance skills and logical reasoning tasks," just as it can lead to "a variety of mental health disorders including anxiety, depression, suicidal behavior, poor self-regulation, alcohol abuse, addiction, and eating disorders" (Madeson, 2023). These are all early signs of chronic depression that can badly affect your wellbeing. But you need to remember that these negative thoughts are more likely to be false, and the more you allow them to grow, the more dangerous they become for your mental, physical, and overall health.

For older people, the biggest disadvantage of loneliness is probably the fact that it can lead to a shorter lifespan. One important study has shown that loneliness "does not just affect an individual's psychological and emotional health; its effects appear to accelerate physiological aging and predict morbidity and mortality" (Madeson, 2023). In this regard, Karaska (2023) has observed that

> [Loneliness] can lead to high blood pressure, stroke and heart disease. It can also double the risk of Type 2 diabetes and raise the likelihood of dementia by 40%. As a consequence, chronically lonely people tend to have an 83% higher mortality risk than those who feel less isolated.

Another important study "cites a meta-analysis that found that the risk of premature death due to loneliness increased by 26% and 29% due to social isolation" (Cherry, 2023). Further, the impact of loneliness on the brain can be really horrible in the long run. It is believed that "Loneliness has been implicated in everything from increased risk of hypertension and heart disease to a reduced antibody response to the flu vaccine" (Colino, 2020). In this regard, researchers have found that "the brain's loneliness hot spot nestles within the default network, a part of the brain that activates when we are mentally on standby" (Karaska, 2023). In addition, the researchers established that

> some regions of the default network are not only larger in chronically lonely people but also more strongly connected to other parts of the brain. Moreover, the default network seems to be involved in many of the distinctive abilities that have evolved in humans—such as language, anticipating the future and causal reasoning. More generally, the default network activates when we think about other people, including when we interpret their intentions.

The findings on default network connectivity provided neuroimaging evidence to support previous discoveries by psychologists that lonely people tend to daydream about social interactions, get easily nostalgic about past social events, and even anthropomorphize their pets, talking to their cats as if they were human, for example.

Researchers across the board agree that loneliness can progressively age the brain, cause people to be unhappy about life, prevent graceful aging, and unfortunately, make anyone die earlier than they were supposed to. Among 1,527 people with Parkinson's disease that participated in a study, it was found that

> Those who answered True to the statement "I am lonely" reported approximately 55 percent greater symptom severity over time. They also had a lower quality of life score. By contrast, participants who had a lot of friends or who were married or in a partnership had a higher quality of life score.

However, this should not be interpreted to mean that people who are married or have intimate partners do not experience loneliness. In fact, researchers have made it clear that loneliness can be divided into three types: collective, relational or social, and intimate or emotional. The researchers have defined emotional loneliness as "the yearning for a close confidante or emotional partner" (Subramanian, 2020). On the other hand, collective loneliness is "the need for a network or community of people with shared purpose and interests," while relational loneliness is "the longing for close friends and social companionship" (Subramanian, 2020). So, while it is less likely for someone who is happily married or with a serious intimate partner to experience emotional loneliness, they can pretty much experience collective or relational loneliness. Practically all aspects of your life will be adversely affected by loneliness, including your ability to function properly in the day and sleep peacefully at night.

BENEFITS OF SOLITUDE

Do not allow society to pressure you into thinking that being alone is bad. There is nothing inherently bad about being alone or solitude. The only time it becomes a problem is when you abuse it. In many ways, solitude is important for your health and general functioning. As much as it is good to spend time with friends in your social circle, it is also highly important to spend time with yourself. The time you spend with yourself is the golden time to be free of the biased eyes of other people. When you give yourself the opportunity to enjoy being alone, you open the doors to many new things that can help you live a happy long life and reduce your risk of becoming lonely. Essentially, you learn more about yourself when you practice healthy solitude or the right dose of being alone. In addition, solitude brings out the best in you by helping stay in touch with your inner self and helping you discover new ways of expressing yourself. It gives you the opportunity to reexamine the decisions you are making at your stage in life, which can significantly help you make better decisions.

When you think of solitude or spending time with yourself, do not think of it as something out of the ordinary that you have to do. Rather, think of solitude as a special time in the unavoidable hours you spend with yourself every day that helps you improve your quality of life. To learn to enjoy solitude and tap into its many benefits, you can start by dedicating a small portion of your time every day to checking in with yourself through silent meditation, mindfulness, and other relevant tools you will come across later in this book. By listening to your inner thoughts in silence and communicating with your emotions mindfully, you will learn to appreciate the connection you are making with yourself and the way it impacts your way of life. This process can also help you develop natural ways of eliminating negative thoughts and emotions.

Additionally, think of any activity you would like to try in your own time, any activity that you do not wish to try in front of other people or that you enjoy more when you are alone. It could be singing, dancing, jumping, reading, writing, knitting, planting flowers, listening to your favorite songs and new ones, watching new movies and tv shows, and practicing solo walking or taking a stroll in nature. In fact, you can train yourself to make a solo walk part of your daily routine. These walks don't have to be long, 10 to 15 minutes should do the trick. This is particularly good for your physical and mental health. Allow yourself to do any of these things as naturally as you can. Do not be afraid of writing bad poems, being goofy, or making mistakes while knitting or doing any other activity. The space is yours and the only person you should focus on is yourself. You can be sure that you will learn more about yourself.

Also, during this process, you can dedicate a portion of your time to speaking positively about yourself and appreciating the stage you are in life. Equally, be vulnerable with yourself, allow yourself to think about and express your emotions, no matter what they are. You can learn more from these emotions. The goal of this process is to help you grow into the fabulous different parts of you that you may have missed out on in the past. It is also a good way of getting used to being old without the negative feeling of chronic loneliness. in fact, the more time you spend with yourself, the more opportunity you will have to develop new routines that will make your life more exciting. This process can help you appreciate the things you have ignored from the past and the things you wish to include in your daily routines now. In all, the most important secret to enjoying solitude is to be flexible with your ideas and rituals. If you feel like changing something, change it. If you feel like trying something new, do it.

Let me also add that your time in solitude should not mean you are cutting yourself off from anyone and everyone completely. In fact, when you take a walk in the morning or at your preferred time, you can go to the park and sit for a few minutes, watching people and just taking in the beauty of the different faces and things you see. It improves your sense of appreciation of life in general and your personal journey in particular. While being alone, you can still stay in touch with the people you love and care about virtually. You can send emails, hop on a call or two, and Facetime a family member or friend from way back. There are older people who lost those close to them without knowing because they were too carried away being alone that they forgot about the people they cared about and loved in the world. Do not make the same mistake. Ultimately, by enjoying and getting used to solitude, you open up the pathways for recharging yourself and coming out of solitude a new version of you every time.

The results of your time in solitude will quickly reveal themselves when you are again in your social circles. For example, according to Morin (2017), spending time with yourself is a good way to improve your ability to be empathetic. This is because the more time you spend with people in your social circle, the more likely it is that you will develop a "we vs. them". But when you practice solitude, "you develop more compassion for people who may not fit into your 'inner circle'" (Morin, 2017). Additionally, some researchers have found that "the ability to tolerate alone time has been linked to increased happiness, better life satisfaction, and improved stress management" (Morin, 2017). In this regard, you can be sure that when you start meeting the people in your community and social circle again, you will most likely feel more energetic and enthusiastic to connect with them. To be able to fully enjoy these results, it is also important that you know when to stop being alone and invite friends over or engage in one activity or the other with your social friends and community. When you stick to a routine of getting the right dose of solitude, you significantly increase your ability to connect better with other people. In general, the more time you spend with yourself, the more you will experience happiness, peace, creativity, better mental health, and a higher level of concentration and daily functioning, particularly when you are engaging with the rest of the world.

CHAPTER 2

BUILDING CONNECTIONS— F.R.I.E.N.D.

"Friendship is born at that moment when one person says to another, 'What! You too? I thought I was the only one.'"
— *C.S. Lewis*

As humans, we thrive off the connections we make. Nurturing friendships and social associations can make our lives more enjoyable and meaningful, especially in our old age. When we have even one good friend with our best interest at heart, the world can seem like a big fertile ground for our dreams and aspirations. In the same way, the lack of wonderful social connections and bad associations can make our lives pretty miserable. Some relationships are good and some are just too awful to keep on. This is why it is really crucial to prioritize nurturing the right relationships. When it is done the right way, the meaningful connections you build can significantly reduce your risk of serious loneliness, unhealthy isolation, and depression.

THE IMPORTANCE OF FRIENDSHIPS

Usually, the right relationships come with a lot of positives. Great friendships provide and enhance strong and reliable support systems, they challenge you to be the best version of yourself, and they help you cope with life's adversities and disappointments. Nurturing beautiful friendships will give you the assurance you need that you are not alone in the world. Often, these friendships will help you see life from a different point of view and increase your sense of appreciation for the things you have been through and what you have achieved for yourself. As older adults, whether you are strengthening old relationships or nurturing new ones, friendships can add more beauty, joy, and good health to your life. They have the potential to help you develop your empathy skills, social skills, listening skills, and other interpersonal skills that you may find difficult to develop on your own.

Due to the many changes that can occur in a person's lifetime, older people may find themselves in a situation where it is hard to maintain old relationships at the same rate as they used to. Your old friends may pass away, move to a new city or faraway country, or you might even grow apart. As humans, our interests change from time to time, and it is fine to express your feelings when you feel like there is a widening gap between you and the people you used to like to spend time with. This does not always mean you have been keeping the wrong people by your side, especially if they have always been nice to you. It could mean that you have simply outgrown what you had with them, and that is likely to happen as you grow older or grow apart. Quality relationships are healthy relationships. The fact that you have them with one person does not mean you will never have them with another. At the same time, the fact that you have a great connection with one person does not mean you have to force the same connection with other people. You can have one great connection and be happy and have multiple friends and be miserable. The most important thing is to put quality connections over the number of friends you have.

In the later years of your life, you will find that the best friends to have around are the ones who can add light and joy to your life as much as you add to theirs. These are the people you can count on when the chips are down, they are the ones that will bring additional beauty to your view of the aging process. You will also find that you feel a different quality of connection with friends with whom you can share interests, stories, and experiences in your old age. Meaningful friendships that progress into or are formed in your old age are usually built on genuine connections, so they have higher chances of helping you connect deeper with your inner self, experience less loneliness or isolation, develop a greater sense of purpose in life. As a result of these friendships, you will find that your mental, emotional, and physical health are benefitting greatly. For example, medical experts have shown that "Patients who were socially engaged tended to have better outcomes despite their complex conditions" (Vengrow, n.d.). Even when you are struggling with one age-related health problem or the other, great friendships and genuine social connections in old age can significantly improve your ability to cope mentally with these challenges. According to Vengrow (n.d.),

> They [older patients] could have diabetes, chronic obstructive pulmonary disease, congestive heart failure, or all three things, and still be doing better because of their improved mental health, their regular social activities, and their dedication to taking care of themselves so that they could continue their regular social activities.

In addition, experts believe that great friendships "can strengthen our immune system, help us recover more quickly from illness, sharpen our memory and even help us live longer" (Vengrow, n.d.). In this regard, one study has found that people with great friends and social connections have up to "have a 50% greater chance of outliving those with fewer social ties" (Vengrow, n.d.). When you think of all the benefits associated with building and nurturing great friendships, you will agree with me that it helps to have one, especially as you grow older. But don't force the process of making friends or forming connections. You stand a risk of making shallow connections if your force the process. There are many natural ways of meeting new people, or even rekindling old relationships. Whether it is at a community center, a gym, public park, or even on internet apps or platforms for older people, you can meet people and form great connections with them.

These relationships are usually built on the values and interest that you share in common with other people. It also means that you are willing to be there for them as much as they are there for you. Great relationships are like two-way streets; it is about giving and sharing. But the more you develop these connections, the happier you will be, and that is good for your health in the long run. In this chapter, we will delve more into the FRIEND framework, which you can use as your guide to building or nurturing you social connections.

F - FIND COMMON INTERESTS

One of the basic things you will want to establish when building new friendships or reevaluating old ones is what we call common interests. These common interests are the hobbies or activities you do with friends and families. They help to build great connections and foster bonding while having massive fun at the same time. Interestingly, these common interests are things you can nurture with not just your friends but your family as well. In fact, many older adults might remember the activities and hobbies they loved doing in their days of youth with siblings and parents. Some families have hobbies that they do as rituals, and these hobbies are cherished by both the young and the old in the family. Some of these hobbies or family rituals include skating, skiing, surfing, fishing, bird-watching, crafting, religious fellowships, movie nights, karaoke nights, and more. Although it is likely that highly physical activities might be difficult to continue in your old age, the easier ones such as fishing or knitting can be done without any hassle. The reason I am mentioning family first is because some older people have the strongest connections in their lives with their siblings, cousins, and other family members. There are also people for whom these family rituals will serve as a great reminder of what it means to share common interests with other people.

At the same time, the act of bonding over shared interests can be really tricky. For example, when some hobbies or activities are not equally loved by people, their bonding can grow weaker over the course of time. In fact, you may have grown up skiing and skating with your family and family friends but realize later that you only did because you always had to participate in the family ritual. You might find out later that you actually enjoy bird-watching, art classes, and knitting more than skating and skiing. This is a good hint that your bond with your siblings or family friends when it comes to shared interests would likely take a dip. Also, this means that you may have to form new connections with people who also enjoy bird-watching, art classes, and knitting. When you think of the import of this realization, you will agree that lasting social connections are built on genuinely shared interests. You cannot pretend to like something forever; it will only last for a while. Once the pretence is gone, frustrations will set in and cloud your happiness in a way that adversely affects your ability to make positive and genuine social connections. So, you will want to make sure you are bonding with people who actually and genuinely share the same interests as you. This will serve as a solid foundation for building your connection, whether you are building a social or intimate connection.

In the same way that those family rituals were important to your family when you were younger, adult rituals play a significant role in building friendships and fostering bonding. Think of situations where couples or friends share less hobbies in common. There is a bigger chance that their relationship will not last, no matter how hard they try. For example, Stephen Betchen, an expert in marriage and family has found that "differences in interests can cause serious relationship problems" (Betchen, 2020). According to Betchen (2020), he once had a client who met a beautiful, educated, and successful lady that he liked for many different reasons. But the client found out that the lady enjoyed skiing a lot, and he did not. This single difference would become the reason Betchen's client did not invest further in the process. When Betchen's client decided to have a discussion with the lady about his decision to put an end to their new relationship, their conversation flowed in this way, starting with the lady's response to his decision:

> "People do not have to share interests. And if I want to ski, I can ski with my friends. You and I can do other things."

> Fair enough, but in retort, my client asked the magic question: "How often do you ski?" Without hesitation, the woman said, "six months of the year." In response, my client told her that he was not trying to be critical of her lust for skiing, and in fact, he admired her for her dedication to her passion. He assumed that her skills were close to that of a professional. The woman did not deny this but reiterated that my client did not have to go with her on her ski trips, and if he did, he could find other things to do. Astutely, and in an effort to exit as gracefully as possible, my client said to the woman: "Picture this: You are skiing on a mountain in Switzerland with Bode Miller (ref. to the great skier) and I am sitting in the ski lodge with a cup of hot chocolate. How long [do you] realistically give our relationship?"

To that my client reported the woman gave no response and disappeared from my client's life.

This little story is a good example of what it means to actually be honest about bonding and sharing interests with other people. If you want a relationship with an intimate partner or your social connections to last, you will want to make sure it is built on genuine shared interests. This does not mean that the only thing that matters in your relationship is your shared interests; it just means that it is a great place to start. When you put some effort into chatting to and knowing the interesting people you meet at community or senior centers, public parks, volunteering events, or leisure walks, you will be able to identify the interests you have and don't have in common. In fact, another good way to meet new people that you can get to know on a deeper level is reading groups. Reading groups, whether physical or virtual, can help you know people better and get to decide those you share interests with and those that you do not. As you grow older, these interests and hobbies may become the pillar holding the rest of your life together. They can become the reason why you are not getting sick or dying from loneliness and depression. They can also significantly increase your happiness, satisfaction, and sense of appreciation, which can help to improve your health and prolong your life.

R - REACH OUT AND COMMUNICATE

For older adults, particularly those who are over 60 years old, friendships can be really complicated. There are two types of older people: the sociable ones and the ones who are not. For sociable older people who are more likely to have had friends for a long time, there is the possibility that their old friendships have been affected by time for different reasons. For example, some older people decide to live with their kids, away from where they have always been, leaving their friends and old relationships behind. This puts the older people moving away and the older people being left behind in a new situation in which building new friendships can appear or become really difficult. In the same way, older people who are not really sociable may experience a greater mental and physical need for social connectedness. For either of the two, one thing is vital: they need to start reaching out more.

Reaching out is simply the attempt you make to build connections with new people or strengthen connections with old friends. After living for more than 60 years on earth, you would expect that most older people would be able to make friends easily. But this is usually not the case. The reason why this happens are many. For some older people, they find it hard to connect with people and tend to think that the only thing that matters at their stage in life is simply waiting for death to take them away. For others, it might be their rigid cultural, social, or political standards that makes it difficult for them to socialize easily or connect with other people. This is usually the case when older people find themselves in a different environment than they used to know. This particular group of older people may have gotten along well with friends who shared the same opinions they are holding on to tightly now, and this may have worked for them because they met those friends when they were young. At old age, a lot of things have changed, including the size of people that older people are constantly exposed to. Unlike the days of youth when there was the colleges, concerts, debate forums, festivals, and so many other platforms for exposure and connection, older people do have the same level of mobility they used to enjoy. So, these can make it more difficult to build new connections.

At the same time, there are useful tips that can help older adults and seniors to build new connections easily. The first tip is to try to keep an open mind. The more flexible you are to meeting people, the more likely it is that you will. But when you are closed off to the possibilities, whether because you have always not been really sociable or because you find it hard to connect with people who don't agree with your opinions, then the chances of meeting new people or reaching out to build new connections will get smaller. Also, it is crucial to the process that you stay positive about reaching out and forming new connections. Do not be held back by negative thoughts that might trick you into thinking that you are a boring person because you are old. The truth is, when you allow thoughts like that to grow, you will never find out if people really think that or not.

From what we know, this is usually not the case and you need to trust more in yourself and your ability to actually find people who share the same values and interests as you do. This requires that you have to be willing to start conversations where there are none. It also requires that you put yourself out there more. In other words, make yourself more accessible by attending more age-appropriate events, joining social groups for seniors, trying activities with other seniors that you will likely not have done if your were indoors. Also, you can reach out to old friends who are alive and well in other districts and check in with them. Show that you care about them while they are still alive. Talk about how much you miss them and share memories about the past that you have missed. You can even plan short trips together to catch up on old times and talk about new excitements.

When it comes to building new connections or strengthening old ones, you should always be willing to make "small talks." Contrary to what you may hear people say, small talks are actually good because they can help you start conversations easily and establish rapport with people. Asking simple questions about activities you find yourself doing with other older people, or exchanging comments about values and interests can go a long way in opening up new doors to lifetime friendships. You can also give compliments, show empathy, mention something you share in common with someone, practice active listening, tell a simple joke or stay funny while trying, and just let your lovely self shine to the people you are meeting. While you are at it, try not to be judgmental; it is likely that the older people you are meeting have seen as much of life as you have, and people have different reasons for the things they believe in and practice.

For example, if you join a book club, you will find that it is easier to talk about a book and the characters or events you find interesting in the book when you are willing to communicate. By expressing yourself, you will find natural allies with whom you can build new relationships. This also applies for other activities or social groups out there that are available to older people. Whenever opportunity allows, you should also chat to younger people; you might be pleasantly surprised by the interests and values you share in common with a much younger person. Whether you are walking, sewing, crafting, gardening, surfing the internet, or volunteering for causes that you care about, you will find that the more you put yourself out there, the more opportunities you will have to meet people and build new connections.

1 - Invest Time and Effort

The time that you invest in nurturing your social connections will prove more beneficial to your overall health and happiness than you can imagine in the long run. As older adults or seniors, you will find that there are many moments you wish to share with someone else as a friend. Moments that help you stay grounded in difficult times, and moments for letting go of all worries that may otherwise affect you mentally. For example, meeting with friends to take a walk with your pets, read a book together, or talk about random stuff can go a long way in strengthening your friendship and bond. You will find those moments you get to share around your social connections to be a blessing and a great way to confirm that you are not alone. The good feeling you get out of those memories can make it much more easier to live every day feeling nice and enthusiastic.

Time and effort go side-by-side. By setting aside the time for social connections in the same way that you allow for solitude, you will find that you feel more grounded, happy, and content with life. For example, you can choose to have a weekly or bi-monthly to-do list with friends and close relatives. Naturally, the human brain is wired in such a way that once you have an exciting event to look forward to, your anticipation and enthusiasm will grow over time. If the first event goes well, it will be easier to host new ones and have even better experiences. The more you stay consistent connecting with your friends in this way, the more you will reassure them that you can make time for them, which is a good way to build trust and bond better. As you spend more time together, you will find common activities that you can do weekly, monthly, or bi-monthly. Sometimes, come up with random ideas to show that you appreciate your friends, just as you know they appreciate you too. For example, you can write them a letter, send them an email, or share something funny you found on the internet with them. These little things can go a long way in strengthening your bond with friends.

In addition, you can organize community events and volunteer opportunities for your friends and the other people in their social circle. These are some of the things my father used to do with his friends. You will find that sharing art classes, taking yoga classes together, beautifying an existing garden (could be yours or theirs), or doing a drive for a cleaner neighborhood can help you feel more alive and happy than you might being alone. There are also health advantages to these physical activities, and the more you do them the higher your chances of avoiding cardiovascular diseases, obesity, and other age-related health problems. Also, you can choose to create or join an online group for seniors with friends and meet other people together. You can also try some brain-stimulating exercises such as board games, card games, sculpting, puzzles, learning something new, and so on.

Importantly, make sure the time and effort you are putting into your relationship is reciprocated by your friends as well. In fact, make sure that you and your friends are practicing reciprocity in a healthy way. To be able to do this, you will want to encourage honest communication between you and your friends. There are different ways to practice reciprocity. According to Morse (2022),

> Reciprocity in relationships is the mutual exchange of energy and support between partners. There are different types of reciprocity: Generalized reciprocity is giving without expecting a specific outcome, balanced reciprocity is an equal give-and-take, and negative reciprocity is unequal. In a healthy relationship, each individual takes turns giving and receiving energy and support, so everyone feels well-loved.

> ...In a relationship with healthy reciprocity, each individual feels they give and receive energy; this feeling of mutual exchange strengthens the relationship overall. On the flip side, a lack of reciprocity can create an unhealthy relationship where one partner experiences burnout or feels used or unloved.

As much as you may be more than willing to invest your time and effort into your social connections, it is also crucial that you get the same or nearly equal amount of time and effort from your friends as well. This exchange of time and effort will go a long way in ensuring your relationship stays positive, healthy, and satisfying. But make sure you do not focus too much on reciprocity in such a way that it hinders you from having fun with your friends and social connections. When practicing reciprocity, Morse (2022) has advised that it is better to "think long-term." What this means is that "In any situation, there will be someone who's giving energy and someone who's receiving energy. Avoid focusing on these specific moments to judge if there's an imbalance" (Morse, 2022). Sometimes, you might just want to do something kind for your friends, and that is perfectly fine. So, while it is crucial to practice reciprocity, it is also helpful to not be too distracted by constantly trying to figure out what is healthy reciprocity and what is not. Also, always let empathy guide your actions with friends and social connections. It is a great way to show that, above all, you are a good human being.

E - EMPATHIZE AND UNDERSTAND

One of the most effective ways to develop a strong bond with your social connections is by constantly showing empathy and understanding. People are different, and friendships are complex. But one thing every human being appreciates is empathy. When you show that you understand people because you have been or are also in their shoes, it fosters closeness and enhances trust. As an older adult, if you have ever struggled with connecting with people, practice empathy and understanding, and you will find that you can get along and form strong connections with just about anybody. By showing empathy and understanding, you are letting the other person know that you see them, hear them, and wish to be there for them regardless. However, empathy and understanding happens only when you actually pay attention to the other person and what they are saying. This is why active listening is really crucial.

Active listening is how you read between the lines of what someone is saying and get them to share how they truly feel with you. All active listeners have some traits in common, and they include the ability to be present in their conversations with other people, the use of positive body language and direct eye contact, encouraging them to open up by asking open-ended questions, and making sure that you are judging them in any way (Cuncic, 2022). When you think of active listening, think of it as a process where you talk a lot less and listen a lot more. This means that you have to be willing to not interrupt them when they are speaking, and you have to be willing to keep an open mind about whatever they say. Sometimes, people just want to give vent to their frustrations and challenges, and other times, they want to feel seen and heard. it could be a problem they are having with their children or grandchildren, and it could be something they have been trying to do but can quite get right. Giving your friends the assurance that they can feel comfortable sharing with you without any judgment and with your complete support is one of the best ways to build genuine connections with people.

At old age, you will find that it is really unnecessary to judge people when you can listen to their story and empathize with them instead. All the moral and political biases that may have seemed really cool to you in your youth may turn out not to be as fantastic as they used to be in old age. This will happen in part because you have joined the league of those people who can practically say they have "seen it all." The advantage of old age is that it affords you the privilege to make wiser decisions. As a result, when building relationships with people, one of the important things you will want to keep in mind is that it is better to empathize and understand rather than criticize and judge. In active listening, you are not listening to argue or impose your opinions and thoughts, you are listening to empathize. The more you can practice your active listening skills with your friends, the more you will learn about them, and the better it will be for your relationship.

Another good way to demonstrate your empathy and understand to your friends is by letting them know you will always be there to support them emotionally. If you can listen actively to what your friends or relatives have to say, then you can also show them that they have your emotional support. This is also a communication skill that you use to reassure your friends that they are not alone. According to Villines

(2022), "Emotional support is showing care and compassion for another person. It can be verbal or nonverbal." Apart from the personal challenges that older people face sometimes, there is a good chance that they will also need emotional support from time to time. It might be because they wish to celebrate something good or express sadness over something bad. Good and bad things happen all the time, and sometimes older people tend to see a lot of both because of how long they have been alive. According to a pertinent study (Villines, 2022),

> More than half of people say that they need emotional support to make difficult decisions. For people with mental or physical health conditions, having the right social support can help improve the quality of life, and may even lengthen it.

Emotional support is all about empathy, compassion, validating, and reassuring. This requires that in addition to listening actively and validating, you can also offer to help with anything they may need that is within your power. How we show up for people also goes a long way in letting them know they have our emotional support. This may be something as simple as talking about a favorite memory that you both share, offering to go for a walk or drive, or any other thing you can do to take their mind away from that pain and help them feel better. But whatever you do, do not minimize their emotions or experiences, and try to follow up with them or recommend that they see their doctor or therapist as well.

The beautiful thing is, emotional support also has a lot of health advantages. According to the 2022 Stress in America report of the American Psychological Association, emotional support can significantly reduce stress and promote overall health. In the report "52% of people who felt that they needed more emotional support during the COVID-19 pandemic said that their life stress had increased, compared with the 27% who reported having adequate emotional support"

(Villines, 2022). So, when giving emotional support to your friends, know that you are not just helping them feel better emotionally but you are also helping them stay healthy. At the same time, keep in mind that you are also allowed to reach out to your friends for emotional support, and if you feel like the support of your friends is not enough, you can contact your therapist or doctor.

Nurture the Relationship

Every relationship is like a flower. If you care for it, it will bloom and bring you peace and joy. If you don't, it will wither and die. As older adults, how you approach the relationships you keep can significantly impact your happiness and sense of satisfaction. By nurturing your social and familial connections, you are creating a lovely environment where your social connectedness can thrive. The fabulous thing about the world we live in now is that you can nurture your relationship without living the comfort of your home. By simply staying connected to the internet, you can grow your relationships and let the people you care about know that you care about them. From phone calls to Zoom video calls, Facetime, and Facebook, older people are currently using different virtual mediums to stay in touch with the people they love and care for. For example, a research by the Pew Research Center has revealed that the number of Americans between the ages of 55 and 91 who use Facebook nearly doubled between 2015 and 2019 (Vogels, 2019). With the COVID-19 pandemic forcing people to stay indoors more, you can be sure that the figure has more than doubled since then. This goes to show that older people are now seeing the benefits of connecting virtually with friends and family who may not be as close or free as they used to be. Importantly, this is a good example of how to nurture relationships.

Apart from checking in, virtual calls and internet platforms can be used for enjoying certain activities together. For example, you can stream a movie online and watch with friends and family. In fact, you can share views and takeaways from the movie afterward, using it as an opportunity to build an even stronger connection. In addition, there are online gadgets and services that make it possible for you to enjoy modern technological devices that are simple and easy to use. For example, Shannon (2020) has suggested tailor-made technological devices and services such as Grandpad and StoryWorth. According to Shannon (2020), Grandpad "has built-in Wi-Fi and allows users to video chat, make audio calls, play games, watch videos, and much more." The amazing thing is that seniors can use Grandpad by without remembering passwords or connecting modem. In the same way, Shannon recommends the online service StoryWorth for preserving beautiful family memories. According to Shannon (2020):

> Once a week, family members will be prompted via email to reflect on a certain topic or share a memory that comes to mind. They can respond either through email or a phone call. After one year, you will receive a collection of priceless family memories and perspectives printed in a high-quality keepsake book.

Essentially, with services like StoryWorth, older adults can zhoosh up their relationships with family and friends. Also, if you like to do things the old-fashioned way, you can write letters to family and friends, and probably exchange letters every week or twice every month. The advantage of this is that it makes your heart grow less weary and helps to significantly reduce the risk of loneliness. In addition, these letters can be used for sharing important events and updates that are worth celebrating with family and friends. According to Hartwell-Walker (2019), you can nurture your relationships by celebrating rituals and milestones together. It is believed that these rituals help to "provide structure and predictability in an unpredictable world, preserve a culture [or practice], help people make important transitions, create memories" (Hartwell-Walker, 2019), and more.

Every year in the United States since 1988, August 21 is celebrated as the National Senior Citizens Day. This is a beautiful celebration you can share with friends and family. In addition, some senior citizens choose to celebrate every additional year they add to their friendship by going to the place they met or a favorite spot they share. Others celebrate Fourth of July or religious rituals by making colorful ribbons, attending community parades and special social gatherings, or organizing documentary and movie nights. Usually, these rituals and milestones are memorable events to look forward to and cherish. The enthusiasm and joy they bring can make life more beautiful and increase your sense of appreciation for our world. These milestones will also make for great stories in the long run. For example, Wilbanks (2017) has shared a beautiful story about her group of school-mom friends that has lasted for almost two decades. They have made plenty of memories and milestones together, and in her story, she wrote:

> We prayed each other through so many things; from problems our children were having at school to illnesses to marital issues. We wept with each other over heart-wrenching circumstances and cried when friends moved away. We celebrated the accomplishments of each other's children, almost as proud as their own parents. We attended birthday parties, graduation parties and wedding showers. We stood with each other at the graveside. As time passed, we celebrated college graduations, first jobs and a few weddings. We even mourned the loss of each others pets.
>
> Our little group is well, little now. There are six of us left. All of us have grown children, the youngest of them will be finished with college soon. We all pretty much live in an empty nest and we have welcomed a new empty nest mom into our fold.

We went from meeting every week to meeting every other week and phased out the scrapbooking. Now we play cards or dominoes. The one thing that hasn't changed is our friendship and the joy we have in sharing and celebrating the milestones in our lives. (Wilbanks, 2017)

D - DEVELOP TRUST AND RESPECT

One of the most crucial ingredients of any outstanding relationship is trust. If you add respect to that, you will find that such relationships can survive almost anything. Every healthy relationship benefits from trust and respect. Trust is not something that can be rushed, but it is achievable with time and effort. When you think of trust in a relationship, all you have to do is remember all the values you hold dear, and the things you would like and would not like someone to do you. Are the people you are bonding with upholding the values you stand for or betraying them? For example, if you value honesty but you meet someone who does not mind telling a lie or two from time to time, especially at an old age, then you will want to question the trustworthiness of that person. When you use your values, likes, and dislikes as the reference point for approaching your relationships or social connections, you will find that it is easier to figure out who can be your friend and who cannot.

At the same time, make sure that you are the epitome of whatever standard you are holding anyone else to. In general, you will find that people bond easily with honest people. The reason for this is that honesty keeps you in the light; you always know what you are getting. But when you deal with someone who does not value honesty, you will quickly find that they also do not value respect. Dealing with someone who is not trustworthy can also be toxic for your mental and overall health. At the same time, you will want to make sure that you have conclusively dealt with any trust issues that you may have. This is important because you will not be able to truly trust someone when you are being held back by your concerns about trusting anyone. If you must, approach your new connections slowly and watch how things develop over time. Also, do not completely rule out seeking the help of a professional or therapist to work with you on your trust issues.

Every other ingredient in the FRIEND framework requires a foundation of mutual trust and respect. Without these two, no real connection can be made with anyone. In fact, there can be no common interests, nurturing, or empathy and understanding without trust and respect between and your friends. In the same way, there can be no trust without respect and no respect without trust. These two go hand-in-hand and can make or mar relationships. Also, friendships that are built on trust and respect are usually able to establish stronger connections and last longer. When there is mutual respect, you will also be able to set and respect healthy boundaries between you and your friends. Friendships without trust and respect will quickly wither and die.

CHAPTER 3

FINDING PURPOSE

"The purpose of life is not to be happy. It is to be useful, to be honorable, to be compassionate, to have it make some difference that you have lived and lived well."
- Ralph Waldo Emerson

What makes life purposeful? If you ask one thousand people this question, there is a chance you will get nearly as many different answers. The reason why this is so is because people find and live their purpose in many different ways. For Ralph Waldo Emerson, the answer is in the quote above. However, there are many people who will disagree with him.

Generally, people believe that if there is something that makes you want to get out of bed in the morning to make some kind of impact, that is probably your purpose in life. For some, it is just one thing, and for others, it can be multiple things. Also, there are those who believe there is only one purpose for them in life: They have a fixed idea of what they should be doing, and they live the rest of their lives trying to live up to it. For others, it can be different things at different stages in life: They usually just "go with the flow" and try to "figure things out" with time. But having a purpose is a critical human need, probably as important as the air we breathe. This is because having a sense of purpose helps us to fill the emptiness in our lives. Researchers focusing on the connection between older people living a life of purpose and enjoying a happy and healthy life have observed that "Having a purpose provides an intrinsic motivation to adopt healthy behaviors as we age, which will help us to achieve positive health outcomes. Thus, promoting PIL is the cornerstone for successful aging and better health outcomes" (AshaRani *et al.*, 2022).

Without a sense of purpose, most people feel lost and miserable. They struggle with everything, and even when they try to have fun, they are never able to shake off the feeling that something is missing in their lives. This feeling can be worse for older people who have worked a certain job all their lives and suddenly have to live the rest of their lives in retirement. So many aging adults are afraid of retirement simply because of this. They find it hard to imagine life in retirement without the regular job they know. Multiple studies have found that Employment provides an avenue for social integration and identity while retirement changes that structure leading to an existential crisis" (AshaRani *et al.*, 2022). In fact, it has been observed that "Questions about life purpose may arise at any time in life, but you may notice that they are especially prevalent during times of transition or crisis—for example, a career or educational change, personal loss, or long-distance move" (Leonard & Kreitzer, n.d.).

This period of transition is the same for older adults coming into retirement. The chief question they usually ask is "What do I do with my life now?" Some older adults come into retirement with a plan of what they want to do for the rest of their lives. Many others either go into retirement without a plan or with a plan they no longer feel confident about. However, having a sense of purpose is all about doing living for something that brings you joy and satisfaction just as much as it helps you make a positive impact in the world. If what you think is your purpose is not making any positive impact in the world, then it is likely not a real purpose. According to Leonard & Kretizer (n.d.), living your real purpose is all about "recognizing your own gifts and using them to contribute to the world—whether those gifts are playing beautiful music for others to enjoy, helping friends solve problems, or simply bringing more joy into the lives of those around you."

In this regard, you can be sure that your sense of purpose does not have to be something gigantic. In fact, what gives you a sense of purpose can be something as simple as taking a ten minutes walk with older people in your community every morning. It can also be something like raising funds for kids in a poor community to get more education or pursue their dreams. According to popular Life Coach Richard Leider, the equation for purpose is (Gifts (G) + Passions (P) + Values (V) = Purpose (P)). This simply means that to truly understand your purpose and live it, you need to understand your talents, values, and passions or issues that make you passionate. According to the Life Coach Tony Robbins, there are two things you must first eliminate to be able to successfully achieve your purpose in life. These are complacency and limiting beliefs. When you get complacent with your comfortable situation in life, you will find it difficult to live a life of purpose even if you are unhappy. In the same way, limiting beliefs can hold you back from living a purposeful life. According to Robbins (n.d.), limiting beliefs "lead to limiting behaviors like fear of failure and self-sabotage." So, instead of thinking about the reasons why you think you are not good enough, which are usually not true, you can start trusting that you can do great things when you put your mind to it. The foundation of finding and living a life of purpose is "Believing that we have no limitations in life" (Robbins, n.d.).

Discovering Your Interests

One of the reasons why it can be difficult to identify your goals in life is if you do not know the things that truly interest you. You are one step closer to living a life of purpose when you know your interests. For example, if you care a lot about kids, it is likely that you will find any cause that makes life better for kids to give you a sense of purpose. You will also feel the same way if you are passionate about the environment: Causes that make the environment safer and better may give you a greater sense of purpose than anything else. One amazing way for older adults to think about discovering their interests is to see the later years of their lives as an opportunity to start life afresh. The truth is, not everyone gets this opportunity. So, after your retirement honeymoon disappears, kick off on the positive note of knowing you have another chance to live life on your own terms. This can serve as a good place to start thinking about the things you enjoy doing; the things that give you joy and a sense of fulfilment that is permanent.

In the process of discovering your interests, you will want to make sure you are keeping an open mind. This is because you might discover some interests you never seriously thought about before, even though they actually align with your values, and that is completely normal. For example, the 40th President of the United States, Ronald Reagan, was a rising Hollywood actor before he switched to politics to make impact in society. He was 69 years old when he became the president of the United States (Gillet & Feloni, 2017). In the same way, American fashion designer, Vera Wang, was a journalist and several other things before she decided to follow her passion at the age of 40 (Gillet & Feloni, 2017). Also, the late American Chef and Television personality, Julian Child, worked in secret intelligence, advertising, and several other things before becoming a sensational chef who introduced Americans to the cuisines of different cultures and countries at the age of 50 (Gillet & Feloni, 2017). So, before you let limiting beliefs stop you from chasing your dreams, think twice and take inspiration from the people who pursued their interests before you, and also think of the fact that you can do anything you put your mind to, especially when you keep an open mind.

Another way to think of discovering your interests is by looking inward. There is a big chance the interests you are looking for are sitting somewhere inside you, waiting for you to locate them. This requires that you take time to search within yourself for the things that actually interest you. You can start by meditating or writing down your feelings and experiences. Through the process, you can embark on a journey of honestly searching yourself and proving unexpected answers to some of the things that bother you the most. Your only goal should be digging deep to list your "gifts" or natural talents. When you identify these, ask yourself if you have put any of the things on the list to use over the years. Usually, the answer is either in the negative or on the lower side. At this point, the next thing you will want to do is find a way to put your gists to good use and creating a purpose out of these gifts or anyone one of them you identify with the most. Sometimes, it takes seeing someone do something or having eureka moments during certain events to understand which of your gifts can be safely described as more important. This is why it is important to stay connected with the world and not isolate yourself. By investing time and effort in building positive social connections, you will soon find the purpose you want to live the rest of your life for. Once you cross the age of 60, there should not be anything left in life to hold you back from following your long-held passions and interests. Establish for yourself a sense of direction and never look back. However, take time to check in with yourself from time to time. Ask yourself questions about your progress and how you feel following your interests and passion. Also, ask yourself if you are making as much impact as you want and make the necessary adjustments where necessary.

At the same time, if you find the process of discovering your interests to be overwhelming for you personally, you can get a close friend or relative to help you. You will be surprised to find that your friends and relatives might still remember some of the things you used to enjoy doing that you did not get the time or opportunity to do because of the many emergencies of life. A simple conversation about the past and the reasons why you used to enjoy doing those things might rekindle the fire or point you in a totally new direction that can be bountifully rewarding. Also, do not shy away from recruiting the help of an expert such as a Life Coach or a Career Expert. There are Life Coaches who specialize in helping older adults who are 60 and above find their purpose in life. By talking and connecting with these experts, you might be able to find the answers you are looking for that you may not have found on your own.

When you finally feel like you have found the interests that can serve your purpose in life, you can either plan on how to use those interests to make impact in the world or how to learn more about the right ways to put those interests to good use. When you discover your interests, do not hesitate to take things further by nurturing them. One remarkable thing about life is that there is always room for improvement. The point I am making is that you should be open to learning more, even though the wisdom you have developed over the years is already in your favor. You can also share your ideas about the direction you want to go in life with your friends. Let them give you their honest feedback and consider them judiciously for the success of your endeavors. If you take this process seriously enough, you will soon realize that your life is filled with undiluted joy and fulfilment because you are finally putting your interests to good use for your own good and for the good of the world.

Exploring New Hobbies

In addition to finding purpose through your interests, you should always keep an open mind about exploring new hobbies. The good news is that your sense of purpose and catching fun by exploring new hobbies will all work together for your ability to ward off loneliness and isolation. For older adults, every additional moment you get to have fun and be happy is a blessing, and the amazing thing is that you get to do these things on your own terms. Your hobbies will serve as another way through which you stay socially active and stay in good shape mentally and physically. As you dedicate more time to your hobbies, you will get to experience a higher level of emotional stability, mental sharpness, and resistance to age-related illnesses.

When it comes to exploring new hobbies, the first most important thing is to be willing to learn. There are many little things you can try out and enjoy. For example, learning a new dance or the dance of another culture can bring a different kind of freshness to your spirits. In the same way, you can start learning a new language, musical instrument, or try painting, drawing, or playing croquet with friends. You can also try yoga for seniors with friends, historical sites, and probably teach history or any fun topic you are good with. Additionally, you can create a scrapbook, start a podcast for seniors, watch the stars as often as you can, get into woodworking and create objects for yourself, your friends, the older people at your senior center if you have one, or the other residents in your community. Do not forget to also try playing pickleball or chess with friends whenever you can. Apart from these, another activity that is becoming more and more popular is citizen journalism. Basically, you can follow up on issues like climate change, weather reports, and any issue that interests you in your neighborhood and send your reports to news platforms and online databases.

Whether you choose to try out one or more of these examples, they are extremely helpful for your mental and physical health. The more you try any of these activities, the more interest you will develop in exploring more. In general, exploring new hobbies is like trying different brands of new clothes or shoes; you can either decide to keep them or just try something else.

THE JOY OF CONTRIBUTING

Nothing gives people a sense of purpose more than the feeling of usefulness. This is especially true for older adults. In your old age, there are not many things that can reassure you that you are still part of the larger society than making positive contributions to your community. As a result, you will want to stay connected to your community and the issues that matter the most to them. The great news is that staying connected to your community is good for the community and you as well. If you can be useful and avoid loneliness at the same time, then that's pretty much a good deal. For example, a simple act of volunteering for a cause or activity in your community has many advantages that can help you live a fulfilling, healthy, and happy life. Whether it is loneliness you want to avoid, or it is your mental health that you want to protect, or your social connectedness and physical health that you want to improve, or you just want to feel useful, a simple volunteering exercise can help you achieve all of them. Also, volunteering is good for your brain health; it will help you put your knowledge to good use, learn new things, and discover new interests.

For older adults who also play a significant role in their family, volunteering can help you increase your family bond if you make it a kind of family ritual. It can one of those things you pass down to your family as a legacy. The good thing is, volunteering is something you can do at your own time and pace, which makes it suitable for older people. At the same time, volunteering can significantly increase your level of happiness. As a matter of fact, researchers are constantly reporting that older adults who volunteer at varying times tend to experience more happiness than those who do not (Gil-Lacruz *et al.*, 2019; Lane, 2021). In fact, it has been reported that "retired and senior volunteers are more protected from the hazards of retirement, physical decline, and inactivity than people of the same age who do not perform volunteer work" (Gil-Lacruz *et al.*, 2019).

Additionally, volunteering promises a lot of fun when you volunteer for the causes or activities that you actually enjoy. It does not matter if you are fundraising and providing aid or relief to some communities or families in need, supporting the local campaign of a politician you believe in, or beautifying your communities during festive seasons. One thing you should not forget to do is have fun and enjoy the moment as much as you can. In this regard, happiness and volunteering are like five and six. Unlike people who do not volunteer, older people who volunteer have a higher chance of staying healthy, living long, and living their sense of purpose. One important study that monitored nearly 13,000 participants of the Health and Retirement Study has shown that

> If someone volunteered for at least 100 hours per year (less than two hours a week) for four years, they experienced reduced risk of mortality, reduced risk of physical functioning limitations, increased amount of physical activity and better psychosocial outcomes. (Lagemann, 2022)

Apart from these, one of the reasons that older adults experience serious loneliness and social isolation is because of negative self-talk and how it adversely affects their self-esteem. However, you can learn to put an end to this unhealthy behavior by volunteering. This is because volunteering can significantly increase your optimism and self-esteem while you are making your community and the world a better place for it. This is because the sense of pride that you feel when you do something nice or when you volunteer is in a class of its own. Another way to think of volunteering is that it is a good way to take your mind off life's issues that may be upsetting you. In that kind of situation, when you volunteer, you are giving yourself the opportunity to free your mind, stimulate your brain, and come back refreshed to the thing you were trying to deal with. That way, you get to prevent frustration and depression.

Importantly, whenever you volunteer, you will find that it improves your sense of belonging and helps you connect better with your community. by volunteering, you give yourself the opportunity to be part of something bigger than you. As you are making your days better through volunteering, you are also making the days and years of other people and your community better. Also, there are volunteering opportunities that may require older people to travel over a short distance to different communities and share their knowledge and experiences. This gives you the opportunity to share your story and feel more connected to people from different backgrounds and the world at large. Because of these opportunities, you will also get to see other places, and feel the beauty of life in a different environment. There are many older people who enjoy teaching, imparting knowledge, promoting education, and fighting for justice and a better society. For example, Hubie Jones did not found the Boston Children's Chorus or BCC until he was 69 years old. Today, the BCC is famous for all the wonderful opportunities it provides to children from different social and economic backgrounds and how it helps them develop artistic talents that can catapult them to greater heights in the future. At 69, there are many older people who would not have bothered to do anything because they feel they are close to the end of life. This is not true; there is so much more you can do. According to Lagemann (2022)

As more people retire, there's a void of skills and expertise based on a lifetime of experience. This collective knowledge needs to be harnessed to add value to the economy and to foster productivity in organizations and build better communities for us all.

In general, volunteering does not have to feel like a chore for older people, and that is why you should carefully choose the group of people you are volunteering with if you are not leading the exercise yourself. For example, the American Association of Retired Peoples (AARP), AmeriCorps, and Senior Corps are some trustworthy organizations running different programs for senior volunteers who are 55 years old and above in American communities. You can choose to volunteer with either of these organizations and decided what arrangement works for you. You do not have to commit to more than you can handle, and you can space your participation.

CHAPTER
"GOOD WILL"

Helping others without expectation of anything in return has been proven to lead to increased happiness and satisfaction in life.

I would love to give you the chance to experience that same feeling during your reading or listening experience today…

All it takes is a few moments of your time to answer one simple question:

Would you make a difference in the life of someone you've never met—without spending any money or seeking recognition for your good will?

If so, I have a small request for you.

If you've found value in your reading or listening experience today, I humbly ask that you take a brief moment right now to leave an honest review of this book. It won't cost you anything but 30 seconds of your time—just a few seconds to share your thoughts with others.

Your voice can go a long way in helping someone else find the same inspiration and knowledge that you have.

Are you familiar with leaving a review for an Audible, Kindle, or e-reader book? If so, it's simple:

If you're on **Audible**: just hit the three dots in the top right of your device, click rate & review, then leave a few sentences about the book along with your star rating.

If you're reading on **Kindle** or an e-reader, simply scroll to the last page of the book and swipe up—the review should prompt from there.

If you're on a **Paperback** or any other physical format of this book, you can find the book page on Amazon (or wherever you bought this) and leave your review right there.

CHAPTER 4

EMBRACING THE JOY OF TIME ALONE

The time you get to spend alone is a wonderful time for reflection. It is a time to look back, take stock, and be grateful for how far you have come. For some people, the beauty of old age is most obvious in solitude. After decades of waking up and joining the rush hour train to work and back, the peace of retirement is bliss. In your solitude, you will probably find that there is more to being yourself than you have ever had the time to explore. As much as there it is fulfilling to have a purpose and be engaged with the community and maintain social connectedness, the being alone has its own special joys that can only be known in constant, intentional solitude. One of the joys of solitude is that it creates a space for you to be with yourself when things are going right and when they are not. It is your safe space, and everyone needs one, especially in old age.

The truth is, the world can be overwhelming. There are many things happening every day that may initially seem unconnected to us. But after some time, we discover that whether we like it or not, those things tend to affect us emotionally and even physically. For example, the news can be really depressing, particularly for those who are passionate about changing the world and leaving it a better place than they met it. Usually, we approach these issues with a dismissive attitude, thinking it's just news. However, the sadness and horrors eventually get to us. For people who care a lot about changing the world, it can be overwhelming to keep learning that bad things are happening around us and in faraway places, or that everything looks hopeless and the world seems to be in autopilot mode. These can become serious emotional and physical stressors, and they can begin to affect your sleep and other everyday pattern. In the same way, people digest family and social issues differently.

Some older people feel responsible for everybody and everything about them. They feel like the world around them will function less without their constant input and efforts. They care deeply about the world, their family, and their friends. They wish for everything to be beautiful and rosy, for everyone or at least their loved ones to always be happy and well. But because things do not always go in this direction, they might eventually become anxious and overwhelmed by the fact that they are not able to do much or help everybody at once. There is nothing wrong with feeling this way once in a while; after all, we are all humans. However, if negative thoughts and hopelessness are not extinguished quickly, they can lead to serious mental and other health problems. This is the reason why it is crucial to first identify your stressors, or the things that cause to be intensely worried or hopeless. When you know these things, you can plan on how to reduce your exposure to them or better cope with them. In this re-gard, creating a safe space is a great way to recharge and feel re-energized to take on the world.

There are different definitions for a safe space. According to Haslam (2018), a safe space can be described as

> a space where dialogues are open and free of judgment or a space that is physically protected from any sort of threat, like discrimination or violence. When thinking about your home, a safe space might be one that creates a feeling of emotional and physical safety.

In general, when you are in your safe space, you should feel safe enough to reflect, break down, let out all the anger and pain you may be feeling, destress, and find inspiration to keep going at the end of the day. You can go into your safe feeling down and out, but when you come out of it, you should feel better. Apart from the feeling of safety that your home may provide, you can create an additional safe space within your home and fully dedicate it to embracing solitude, meditation, and reinvigoration. This additional space can be anywhere of your choice, but it is best to make it your special safe space only. in this regard, Haslam (2018) has suggested that

> You can turn one area of your home into a meditative space, free from distractions and stimuli, in much the same way you separate rooms for sleeping, eating, and showering. Your safe space should be clearly defined so that your brain learns to associate it with a sense of calm and relaxation. Try and resist the urge to use your med-itative space for work or leisure.

For some seniors, simply having a clean space with no ex-posure to potential physical hazards is enough for them to feel like they are in their safe space. This is one of the reasons why it is important to have an helper or two, whether family or not, to provide support in your retirement and old age. Pre-paring your home to make it feel more like a real safe space can take some redecoration. The older you get, the more careful you have to be in setting your immediate environment. Anything that can trigger a fall, such as a slippery floor cover, loose cords and wires, or a heap of messy stuff lying around must be completely removed. In your bathroom and around your home, you can install grab bars to hold on. You can also install alarm systems and make sure you have your emergency lines on speed dial. A safe space is not complete until you can see as an external extension of who you are. The key is to redecorate your home in a way that speaks to your inner self. There is a special feeling of comfort and reassurance that comes from knowing you are in a space created solely for your safety, peace, and happiness.

ACTIVITIES FOR SELF-REFLECTION

Once you have your safe space set up, it is important to get familiar with it. What you want to achieve is to get so used to your safe space that it becomes your natural place of escape. One of the reasons why this is good is that it helps a lot in self-reflection. Your ability to self-reflect can significantly improve how you get through the most difficult days while also inspiring you to take on new challenges and opportunities. Self-reflection provides an opportunity to acknowledge your previous challenges, the lessons you learned from them, and the resilience you developed along the way. By reflecting on past experiences, you can gain a deeper understanding of your strengths and weaknesses and foster a greater sense of self-awareness. One of the primary purposes of self-reflection is to open your eyes to knowing more about who you are and what has changed about you. It helps you develop insights about the next steps to take, the things to avoid and how to avoid them, as well as the goals you need to set to guide your future actions. It is believed that "when we engage in self-reflection, we're developing what is known as an inner witness. This is the ability to look at yourself—even your own thoughts and even what is beneath the thoughts and emotions—from a slight distance" (Habash, 2022).

In addition, you can learn to practice gratitude through self-reflection. Many times we get carried away by the things we are chasing or involved in that we forget to appreciate the things we have been able to achieve. Through self-reflection, you can develop a stronger sense of appreciation for your accomplishments and milestones in life. Also, it provides a fantastic opportunity to acknowledge your positive contributions to your family, friends, social connections, and the causes you care about. By acknowledging your achievements, you can boost your self-esteem and feel a deeper sense of fulfillment in the legacy you have created. At the same time, self-reflection provides an opportunity for you reevaluate your journey, acknowledge your mistakes and grow from them. You will also be able to better identify the patterns of behavior or decisions that may have hindered your personal growth in the past. By acknowledging these areas for improvement, you can make deliberate efforts to change and evolve, which can help you build a more resilient spirit for personal development.

Think of self-reflection as a powerful tool that you can use to embrace your journey so far in life, to celebrate the wins and the accolades, and to let go off negativities and limiting thoughts. Research has shown that "we think more than 50,000 thoughts per day, of which more than half are negative and more than 90% are just repeats from the day before" (Ackerman, 2017). Think of it as a transformative process that promotes inner peace, personal growth, complete happiness, resilience, and fulfillment. Also, think of the activities you embark on during your self-reflection period as a way to re-imagine and better understand your purpose in the stage you are in life. These activities can help you develop a deeper understanding of your values and aspirations and a vision of the things that truly matter. They can also help you determine what to do and what not to do in any given situation. In fact, self-reflection is a great way to align your old and newfound interests and set milestones for making the most impact you can while alive. According to Habash (2022), "There's an infinite capacity to self-reflect within us, and regular, consistent self-reflection with support can deepen your process of personal and spiritual growth and transformation."

At the same time, it is important to identify the right activities or exercises you can do for self-reflection. There are exercises you can do in your private safe space and the ones you can do in collaboration with close friends, family members, and members of your community. For example, on your own, you can commit to daily self-reflection for 15 or 30 minutes, depending on how much time you can dedicate to the process. You can ask yourself questions like: "How much did I achieve today?" "Did I achieve my daily goals?"; and more. If you were able to achieve your daily goals, ask yourself if there are lessons to draw from that achievement. If not, ask yourself what hindered you from achieving the goal. These questions may not always be comfortable, but the most important thing is to ask and try to answer them. According to Ackerman (2017), other questions you can ask yourself during self-reflection are:

✧ Who am I, really?

✧ Why do I matter?

✧ How will I live, knowing I will die?

✧ What worries me most about the future?

✧ What am I really scared of?

✧ If not now, then when?

✧ Have I done anything lately that's worth remembering?

✧ Have I made someone smile today?

✧ If I had to instill one piece of advice in a newborn baby, what advice would I give?

✧ Would I steal to feed a starving child?

✧ When did I last push the boundaries of my comfort zone?

✧ What do I need to change about myself?

✧ What do I want most in life?

✧ What is life asking of me?

✧ What's the one thing I'd like others to remember about me at the end of my life?

✧ When all is said and done, what will I have said more than I've done?

✧ When all is said and done, what will I have said more than I've done?

Apart from the above questions, other questions you can ask, according to Ackerman (2017), are:

✧ What is my favorite way to spend the day?

✧ If I could talk to my teenage self, what is the one thing I would say?

✧ Who are the people in my life who genuinely support me?

✧ If my body could talk, what would it say?

✧ What do I love about life?

✧ What is the most surprising thing about my life?

✧ What's the one topic I need to learn more about to help me live a fulfilling life?

✧ What are the things I would like to say 'no' to?

✧ What are the things I would like to say 'yes' to?

✧ What are the words I need to hear?

You can introduce a little fun into the process of asking and answering these questions by creating a reflection wheel with different colored spaces for each of the questions. Your colored reflection wheel can also teach you to take responsibility for your actions in ways you may not have thought about before. You can also create a surface in your safe space for using a single word on sticky notes to describe your day or different parts of your day. In the same way, you can create a monthly reflection exercise or a detailed pattern of self-reflection yearly or twice in a year, in addition to your daily reflection exercise.

Additionally, journaling is a good strategy for self-reflection in your safe space. It helps you to recount events and explain their meaning in words that you may not even be aware was in your thoughts. Journaling is way of drawing yourself out of your inner comfort zone and opening up to yourself in a way that intensely fosters self-awareness. Also, journaling can help you quickly identify your mistakes and develop ways to correct them and prevent reoccurrence in the future. Remember, the goal is not to blame yourself or make yourself feel worthless. The goal is to develop insights and learning strategies for becoming a better person in your old age.

GROWING THROUGH SOLITUDE

Solitude, unlike loneliness, fosters personal growth and self-awareness. The things you learn when you are alone and engaging your mind can make a significant difference in the quality of your life. Solitude takes away the distractions of life and enriches your daily experience, particularly your daily experience as a senior or older adult. It also gives you a better opportunity to grow emotionally and depend less on other people for emotional happiness. For example, if you answer some of the questions above sincerely, you will find that you will be proud of the version of you that you have discovered. You will find that you are able to decide more easily what you need and what you don't need to put your effort into, or who and who you do not need to get involved with. As older adults, your need for companionship or genuine connection can also make you vulnerable. However, when you have a system of self-regulation such as the time you spend in solitude, you will find that you are able to make better choices in association and socialization. Solitude also teaches you to find comfort in silence; to feel reassured in the calmness of your own voice, paying deliberate attention to no one but yourself. You will find that your sense of direction will, in addition to several other things, improve as a result.

Further, solitude helps you grow because it helps you understand the voices of other people better. For example, if you are reading a book in the quietness of your safe space, the book tends to have a more profound meaning than when you are reading in a noisy or busy environment. In the same way, if you are listening to a podcast or meditation sound, you will find that you are able to analyze every word or sound you hear in a really deep way that helps you connect your mind and soul. Our mind benefits more from our reflections in solitude. It is like the magical key to unlocking the treasures hidden away in the depth of our soul. Also, solitude does not have to be confined to your safe space indoors. You can be outdoors, in a very quiet place like a garden, and still enjoy the blessings of solitude. Apart from the many ways it improves your personal life, solitude also helps you connect with other humans better. It helps you become a better listener, makes your intuition better, and develops your ability for empathy and compassion.

When you are with family or other people you love after being alone, you get to appreciate your relationship with them in new lights. Also, spending time alone helps to sharpen your mind and make you more creative in ways you may never have known you could before. This is especially vital for health and longevity of older people. The human mind age as we grow older, and giving yourself the opportunity to reflect and reawaken your inner self is a good way to constantly stimulate your mind. Another great result of such commitment is that you will become more productive in your endeavors and happier in spite of life's challenges. You will go through different phases in your later years that will make you doubt a lot of things, including the point of being alive and living. But by connecting more with yourself through solitude, you will find more peace and feel more reassurance about the quality of your life. Also, the quality of how you engage with other people will likely improve after spending time in solitude.

Solitude is something you can do at your own pace and time, especially if you are an extrovert. But you will find that the more time you spend getting to know yourself, the more likely you are to get to know other people better. We are creatures of habits, so even if spending time alone is a bit of struggle in the beginning, do not give up and trust that you will come to enjoy every bit of it the more you practice. Remember, solitude is not an opportunity for you to completely isolate yourself from the world and put yourself at risk of chronic loneliness and depression. On the contrary, solitude is how you improve your health, sense of purpose, happiness, and the quality of your life and relationships in general. At the same time, while our minds need peaceful solitude to reflect and grow, our bodies need care and attention to thrive.

CHAPTER 5

Keeping Active and Healthy

"Take care of your body. It's the only place you have to live."
- Jim Rohn

Everything about life in old age depends on good health. If the health is bad, life will be far from fulfilling and satisfying. Due to old age, older people are at a greater risk of getting sick or suffering age-related illnesses. This is because the immune system gets weaker as we grow older. But there are also many old people who are living in good health and enjoying life. There are also old people breaking boundaries and living well beyond the 100-year mark. This is mostly because they have committed themselves to certain lifestyles and health decisions that make them less vulnerable to age-related diseases and weaker immune systems. You can also do the same thing. In fact, you have to do the same thing to live a long, happy life.

If you pay attention to every old adult in good health, you will find that they take self-care seriously and limit or completely stay away from practices or habits than can adversely affect their bodies. This is simply the secret to staying healthy: it is about making healthy choices and staying away from unhealthy habits. But this also requires practicing self-restraint. Many times people do unhealthy things to justify the things they have been through or are going through in life. Sometimes, it is not difficult to understand the reason why, but for the most part, it is possible to develop a healthy habit, in spite of the challenges of life. Also, if your goal is to live long and healthy, they you will want to take self-care and keeping active seriously. This does not reduce the quality of your life, if anything it add to it and makes it better.

There are many tools, recommendations, and options for older people to stay active and healthy. When you inculcate these lifestyle enhancing options into your routines and lifestyle choices, you give yourself the opportunity to live longer and make more positive contributions to the world. For some, it is the joy of spending more time with their families that motivates them to stay healthy and active. Whatever may be your reason, you benefit more from living healthy in a way you will never benefit making unhealthy choices. Every single part of your body is connected to another in ways that they always share in the good and the bad. Apart from people who are born with certain health conditions, the rest of humanity can make healthy decisions for themselves that will make life more soothing, fulfilling, worth the effort in the long run. Without good health, you will not be able to fully benefit from the great tips and suggestions in this book. You will also be unable to make certain daily choices that can enhance your experience of old age and the aging process in your later years. By keeping active and making healthy decisions, you get to redefine the boundaries of your health and the limits of your experiences in life.

EXERCISE FOR SENIORS

When older adults or seniors exercise regularly, they stand to benefit from a wide array of advantages. From mental health to stronger immune system, increase in enthusiasm, stronger interest in socializing, improved stability, and overall wellness. Regular exercise for seniors also improve brain health, cardiovascular health, and mental agility. In fact, the Alzheimer's Research & Prevention Foundation_has revealed in a study that "exercising regularly helps to reduce your risk of developing Alzheimer's disease or dementia by nearly 50%" (Senior Lifestyle, 2020). Also, exercising can delay several age-related bodily decline in older adults and significantly improve your mood and mental approach to life. According to the Centers for Disease Control and Prevention (CDC), the only thing worse than a little exercise is not exercising at all. The CDC recommends "At least **150 minutes a week** (for example, 30 minutes a day, 5 days a week) of moderate-intensity activity such as brisk walking or 5 minutes a week of **vigorous-intensity activity** such as hiking, jogging, or running" (CDC, 2021). Depending on the advise of your doctors, you can also try "At least **2 days a week** of activities that strengthen muscles and activities to improve balance, such as standing on one foot" (CDC, 2021). In fact, the American Senior Communities (ASC) observed in 2014 that

> As we age, our muscle mass begins to decrease. When we enter our forties, adults can lose 3-5% of muscle mass with each subsequent decade of life. Muscle is an essential contributor to our balance and bone strength; it keeps us strong. Without it, our mobility and independence become compromised.

At the same time, because of the impact of regular exercise on the body of seniors, research has shown that "Regular exercise by seniors may decrease the time it takes for a wound to heal by 25%. Also, a healthy, strong body can better fight off infection and makes recovery from illness or injury easier"

(ASC, 2014). The stronger the immune system, the more you can expect your life expectancy to increase. In addition, a study by the Harvard Medical School has revealed that "regular exercise promotes an older adult's ability to walk, bathe, cook, eat, dress, and use the restroom. If self-reliance is a priority, exercise is one of the best ways to maintain independence for older adults" (Senior Lifestyle, 2020). This goes to the heart of one of the most common problems that older adults face. Without the help of an au pair or nurse, many older adults cannot perform basic daily functions. However, by staying committed to a regular exercise routine, they can keep the muscles strong and improve their balance.

Whether you are a senior starting an exercise routine as a beginner or you have been exercising for some time, there is always something for you to do that matches your age and health conditions. For example, 65-year-old Vera Teachout and 73-year-old Cheri Hunt are doing remarkable things in the fitness world. They are both active and are known for their commitment to visiting the gym several times a week. They both look younger and healthier, and they have age-appropriate programs that help to prevent unexpected hazards (Fitting Fitness In, 2021). According to Senior Life (2020), you can try water aerobics exercises such as "flutter kicking, leg lifts, standing water push-ups, aqua jogging, or arm curls," and it is believed that these exercises are "ideal for those living with arthritis and other forms of joint pain, as the buoyancy of the water puts less stress on your joints." Further, it has been observed that "water brings natural resistance, which eliminates the need for weights in strength training" (Senior Life, 2020). In the same way, "Water aerobics exercises improve your strength, flexibility, and balance with minimal stress on your body" (Senior Life, 2020). Apart from water aerobics, you can also try Pilates, which is a "low-impact form of exercise" in which "breathing, alignment, concentration and core strength are emphasized, and typically involves mats, pilates balls, and other inflated accessories to help build strength without the stress of higher-impact exercises" (Senior Life, 2020).

In your Pilates exercises, you can try the "side circles, food slides, step ups, mermaid movement, or leg circle" (Senior Lifestyle, 2020). These exercises can be done with friends, a Pilates instructor, or a fitness expert. Other workouts for seniors include body weight workouts, which can be very beneficial to your muscle strength and prevent the weakening of muscles. Examples of body weight workouts include "step up, bird dog, lying hip bridges, side lying circles," and experts believe they are best done on a mat (Senior Life, 2020). Equally, experts have recommended strength training exercises because they help to "alleviate the symptoms of diabetes, osteoporosis, back pain, and depression, while helping you manage your weight. Strength training also contributes to a higher metabolism and enhanced glucose control" (Senior Life, 2020). Examples of strength training exercises include "Overhead press, bicep curl, tricep extension," and so on. However, it is better to try these exercises under the guidance of a professional or senior workout club. If you must do these exercises yourself, try to avoid "bench press, leg press, abdominal crunches, rock-climbing, high-intensity interval training" (Senior Life, 2020), and other exercises that are too intense for your age. You can discuss your workout routine with your doctor to make sure you are only doing the exercises that are appropriate for your age.

In general, it is better to prioritize consistency over intensity. The most important things is body movement, stretches, and strength training. When you begin to do the exercises in this category, do not overstretch yourself inappropriately and always take things slow. According to some experts, there are multiple exercises you can do within the comfort of your home without putting yourself at too much risk. According to Kilroy (2014), examples of low-intensity exercises you can do on your own include shoulder and upper back stretch, which you can probably do very well if you "bend your right arm, raising it so your elbow is chest level and your right fist is near your left shoulder" (Kilroy, 2014). Then, "Place your left hand on your right elbow and gently pull your right arm across your chest" (Kilroy, 2014). Maintain that position for about 30 seconds before switching to your opposite arm and repeating the same routine. Also, you can try ankle rotations, which requires that when you are "seated in a chair, lift your right foot off the floor and slowly rotate your foot 5 times to the right and then 5 times to the left" (Kilroy, 2014). When you are done with your right foot, you can also switch to your left foot and repeat the same.

For Kilroy, there are two basic stretches that older adults can also try out. The first is the neck stretch, which helps to "relieve tension in the neck and upper back," and the second is the upper back stretch, which helps to "relieve tension in the shoulders and upper back" (Kilroy, 2014). You can use the following instruction for the upper back stretch, according to Kilroy (2014):

✧ Sit in a firm chair. Place your feet flat on the floor, shoulder-width apart.

✧ Hold your arms up and out in front at shoulder height, with your palms facing outward and the backs of your hands pressed together. Relax your shoulders so they're not scrunched up near your ears.

✧ Reach your fingertips out until you feel a stretch. Your back will move away from the back of the chair.

✧ Stop and hold for 10 to 30 seconds.

✧ Repeat 3 to 5 times.

Also, you can use the following instruction for the neck stretch, according to Kilroy (2014):

✧ Stand with your feet flat on the floor, shoulder-width apart. Keep your hands relaxed at your sides.

✧ Don't tip your head forward or backward as you turn your head slowly to the right. Stop when you feel a slight stretch. Hold for 10 to 30 seconds.

✧ Turn to the left. Hold for 10 to 30 seconds.

✧ Repeat 3 to 5 times.

In addition, a simple body movement or pace up and down the room for 10 to 15 minutes can help improve blood flow and circulation. Also, you can improve your health by simply dancing. Dancing is a good cardiovascular exercise that works well for different parts of your body and keep your heart working at a healthy pace. According to Tavel (2021), "moving your body (including your hips) with continuous dancing definitely counts as cardio. Dancing not only elevates the heart rate, but also improves balance, strengthens multiple large muscle groups and lifts your spirits." Another good exercise you can try at home is what Tavel (2021) calls the "sit to stand" exercise, which can greatly help with simple body movements and balance. For this exercise:

> Start by sitting in a chair with a seat high enough that you don't need to use your hands to rise. Have a second chair in front of you for safety. When you're ready, stand up and sit down repeatedly. If it's too challenging, place a cushion or two on the seat to create a higher surface. Repeat 10 times.

Another exercise you can try at home on your bed is the "Bridge" exercise. Tavel (2021) has explained that the Bridge exercise "strengthens the gluteal muscles, which are essential for getting up from a chair, bed mobility, standing, and walking. It also stretches the hip flexor muscles which can become tight and weak from a sedentary lifestyle." To do this exercise, all you have to do is "Lie on your back on your bed with your knees bent and feet flat on the mattress. Raise your hips and hold for three seconds at the top of the motion. Lower your hips. Repeat 10 times" (Tavel, 2021). When doing this exercise, you should also make sure the palms of your hands are facing the mattress. For better flexibility, you can try the Knee Extension stretch, which "helps improve your ability to straighten your knee during walking and avoid the development of a crouched gait. It can also help reduce low back pain by lengthening the muscles that attach to the pelvis" (Tavel, 2021). To do this exercise, follow this instruction (Tavel, 2021):

> Sit upright in a chair and prop one heel on a low stool in front of you. Gently lean forward as you hinge at your hips, feeling the stretch in the back of your knee. Hold the stretch for 1 to 3 minutes before switching legs and repeating on the other side.

To aid you in your exercises, you can get a pedometer or step-counter to track the number of steps you take when you do a short low-impact walk every day. Apart from your walks, a pedometer is a great instrument for tracking your general health condition in relation to your workout progress. For example, in addition to tracking your daily steps, you can also use it to track the quality of your sleep and heart health. This will give you a suitable information with which you can update your doctors. The good news is, there are smartwatches and wristbands with full pedometer functions you can acquire for daily or regular use. You can follow-up with your physical therapist or doctor to confirm what type of pedometer is appropriate for you. Some of these devices already have stopwatches installed in them, which makes them even more suitable to your needs. However, if it's your preference, you can also add a stopwatch to track and time your exercises during workout.

NUTRITIONAL NEEDS

Nearly everything about you declines as you grow older. In your old age, everything about your body becomes more and more delicate. Nutrient deficiencies, which is another sign of aging, can only worsen this natural process. For example, osteoporosis, a sign that your body lacks vitamin D or calcium, is a common age-related condition among seniors. In fact, experts have found that roughly "20% of elderly people have atrophic gastritis, a condition in which chronic inflammation has damaged the cells that produce stomach acid" (Raman, 2017). In addition, research has shown that "Low stomach acid can affect the absorption of nutrients, such as vitamin B12, calcium, iron and magnesium" (Raman, 2017).

According to the Office of Disease Prevention and Health Promotion (ODPHP), "Older adults generally have lower calorie needs, but similar or even increased nutrient needs compared to younger adults. This is often due to less physical activity, changes in metabolism, or age-related loss of bone and muscle mass" (DeSilva & Anderson-Villaluz, 2021). As a result, taking measures to roll back the extreme effects of the aging process is extremely important. So, apart from exercising regularly, another great way to make sure you are staying healthy is by eating healthy.

Generally, older adults need to stay away from sodium, added sugar, and saturated fats while "eating more fruits, vegetables, whole grains, and dairy" can go a long way in improving the quality of their diet (DeSilva & Anderson-Villaluz, 2021). Also, research has shown that older adults, particularly those who are 71 years old and above, do not eat enough protein, which helps to "prevent the loss of lean muscle mass" (DeSilva & Anderson-Villaluz, 2021). In fact, research has shown that "the average adult loses 3–8% of their muscle mass each decade after age 30" (Raman, 2017). However, to improve the quality of protein in the diet of older adults, experts believe that "seafood, dairy and fortified soy alternatives, beans, peas, and lentils are great sources of protein" (DeSilva & Anderson-Villaluz, 2021). Apart from the fact that a higher intake of fiber-rich diet helps with emptying the bowels, experts believe that "a high-fiber diet may prevent diverticular disease, a condition in which small pouches form along the colon wall and become infected or inflamed. This condition is especially common among the elderly" (Raman, 2017).

These protein sources also provide additional nutrients, such as calcium, vitamin D, vitamin B12, and fiber" (DeSilva & Anderson-Villaluz, 2021). Additionally, experts have observed that as we grow older, our ability to sense the need for food and fluids gradually declines, so it is crucial for older adults to have a routine for eating quality diet and also drink plenty of water. In addition, "unsweetened fruit juices and low-fat or fat-free milk or fortified soy beverages can also help meet fluid and nutrient needs" (DeSilva & Anderson-Villaluz, 2021). Further, older adults are expected to take fewer calories, but they also have to compensate for it by taking the recommended amount of other vital nutrients. This is really crucial to avoid malnutrition and serious health complications. For example, researchers have found that "5-10% of elderly people living in a 'community setting' are malnourished; [and] about 60% of hospitalized older adults and anywhere from 35 to 85% in long-term care facilities are experiencing malnutrition" (Homewatch, CareGivers).

In addition, it has been observed that a higher intake of vital nutrients such as Omega-3 fatty acids "can lower heart disease risk factors like high blood pressure and triglycerides"; Potassium helps to maintain "lower risk of high blood pressure, kidney stones, osteoporosis and heart disease", as well as iron and magnesium can go a long way to strengthen the immune system of older adults and increase life expectancy (Raman, 2017). To increase your chances of eating healthy and appropriately, it is advisable to consult your doctor from time to time.

REGULAR HEALTH CHECK-UPS

Regular health check-ups is becoming more popular these days. The reason why this is vital in the aging process is that it helps in detecting life-threatening medical conditions early and taking preventive measures to deal with them. Because of our vulnerability to different kinds of age-related diseases, it is important to do regular health check-ups. Even when we make the best of decisions in terms of our lifestyle and dietary choices, there may be hereditary health conditions we never knew about that can shorten our lifespan if we don't detect them early. The main advantage of knowing about any health conditions early is that you give yourself the opportunity to treat those conditions early or adjust your lifestyle accordingly. By taking your health check-ups seriously, you are potentially increasing your life expectancy and reducing your risk of spending a gigantic chunk of your retirement savings on medical treatments.

The good news is, when you try to do these tests early, some of them are being done for free across the country. In this regard, you need to keep in touch with your doctor to know what tests you need to do annually and what tests, if any, you need to do more frequently. According to Shiel (2018), preventive care can be grouped into three different categories, and they are: Primary prevention, which "includes interventions that can completely prevent the disease in people at risk, [e.g.] immunizations against certain vaccine-preventable diseases such as measles and tetanus"; Secondary prevention, which "identifies established risk factors for disease... in which identifying abnormal results can lead to effective interventions that may prevent serious disease from developing"; and Tertiary intervention, which "is a process for optimizing health once a disease has been diagnosed. An example is a management plan to prevent a person from having another heart attack once they already have established heart disease" (Shiel, 2018). Aging adults, particularly those who are above 50, and older adults should always ask their doctors the following 50 questions, according to Firman (2019):

- ✧ How much physical activity should I be getting?
- ✧ Why are my energy levels so low?
- ✧ How are my nutrient levels?
- ✧ How are my vitamin D levels?
- ✧ How is my blood sugar?
- ✧ What should I be eating?
- ✧ Should I get my lean mass tested?
- ✧ How is my bone health?
- ✧ Do I have a food intolerance?
- ✧ Why is my skin so dry?
- ✧ What can I do about my age spots?
- ✧ What's up with all my skin tags?
- ✧ What can I do between appointments?
- ✧ Which screenings do I need?
- ✧ How often should I get a colonoscopy?
- ✧ How often should I get a mammogram?
- ✧ Why am I waking up during the night?
- ✧ Why am I so sleepy during the day?
- ✧ Is my sleep schedule normal?
- ✧ Are there any alternatives for my medications?
- ✧ Do I really need all these medications?
- ✧ Which vaccines do I need?
- ✧ How is my thyroid function?
- ✧ Can I get lab work done?
- ✧ Can I get labs done on my gut microbiome?
- ✧ Is my digestion normal?
- ✧ How often do I need to see the doctor?
- ✧ Should I see a specialist?

✧ Why am I feeling depressed?

✧ Why am I gaining weight?

✧ Do I need to check my heart health?

✧ Do I need to be tested for STDs?

✧ Why am I having such bad heartburn?

✧ Can I get my moles checked?

✧ Why is my memory so bad?

✧ Should I be worried about dementia?

✧ What can I do to keep my brain sharp?

✧ How can I protect my vision?

✧ What's up with my back pain?

✧ How can I manage my slow metabolism?

✧ How much alcohol is too much alcohol?

✧ Why is my libido down?

✧ Can I balance my hormones?

✧ Why is my bladder out of control?

✧ What can I do about hair loss?

✧ How can I manage my anxiety?

✧ How can I keep my skin healthy and youthful?

✧ Why do I have so many varicose veins?

✧ Should I be taking probiotics?

✧ How can I better combat stress?

Essentially, cancer screenings are important, and so are immunizations, hearing and vision screenings, as well as other preventive screenings. Also, some experts recommend that men who are 50 and above should get health check-ups for Prostate Specific Antigen (PSA) and Prostate Exam to detect prostate cancer early, while women who are 40 and above should do mammogram and osteoporosis screening, as well as pap smear and pelvic exam (Eure, 2023). In addition, the United States Preventive Services Task Force (USPSTF) has recommended regular check-ups for "height loss, weight loss, blood pressure, blood work, electrocardiogram (EKG), colonoscopy, and fecal occult blood test" (Eure, 2023).

For every test, check-up, or screening you go for, always request a copy of the results so you can take them home and add to your medical records file. You should organize these records in a way that is easier for you to easily access any relevant information whenever you need to. For example, you should in your possession vital information like your past and future doctor appointments, medications and dosages, health insurance details, emergency contact list, history of any screenings, addictions, allergies, medications, surgeries, treatments, and so on. Make your medical records file as comprehensive as possible, and make sure it covers your own medical history, your family medical history, and any health complications you may have experienced recently.

You can also store the information digitally on your personal or family computer, or get your caregiver (or assistant, if you have one) to help you with it. This makes it easier to organize and recover any emergency medical information when necessary. You will find that the process is extremely helpful. This will help you stay up-to-date with everything that has to do with your health. If you have a caregiver or personal assistant, this is one of the vital things you should do with them. Also, keeping your medical records helps to save your time and your doctor's time when you need the information. There is no shame in doing regular check-ups, the real shame is in not dealing with a medical condition early when you could have done so by going for health check-ups.

CHAPTER 6

Strategies for Mental Wellbeing

"The greatest weapon against stress is our ability to choose one thought over another."
— *William James*

As older adults, mental wellbeing is vital to your overall health and life expectancy. However, there are many challenges that can hinder your pathway to mental wellbeing, and without the right strategies, everything can become overwhelming very quickly. Generally, older adults are at a higher risk of perceived and real vulnerability in any society (Langmann, 2022). In many ways, this is a worrying fact to deal with at old age, but it also goes to show how important it is to pay attention to your mental health as you grow older. According to the Centers for Disease Control and Prevention (CDC), about "20% of people age 55 years or older experience some type of mental health concern. The most common conditions include anxiety, severe cognitive impairment, and mood disorders (such as depression or bipolar disorder)" (CDC, 2020). In fact, statistics show that in the U.S., suicide is higher among older men compared to any other age group: "Men aged 85 years or older have a suicide rate of 45.23 per 100,000, compared to an overall rate of 11.01 per 100,000 for all ages" (CDC, 2020).

During the COVID-19 pandemic, older adults experienced serious mental health challenges, and those with existing mental health conditions experienced different levels of exacerbation in their condition (Cocuzzo *et al.*, 2022). For example, in China, "37.1% of seniors experienced symptoms of depression and anxiety during the COVID-19 pandemic with those most vulnerable to the effects of depression and anxiety being women" (Cocuzzo *et al.*, 2022). Further, it was reported that severe sleeping problems, as well as mental health challenges such as anxiety and depression were common among older women, particularly the women who lived alone as a result of divorce or loss of their spouse (Cocuzzo *et al.*, 2022). From all that we know about how the aging process affects older people differently, it is clear that seniors need to take their mental wellbeing seriously. Apart from the unavoidable physical changes in old age, it is crucial to stay mentally strong in a world that is still struggling with ageism and bias against older people (Langmann, 2022).

In America, research has shown that depression is "the most prevalent mental health problem among older adults" (CDC, 2020). The adverse effects of depression can be extremely brutal on older people, especially if they already have a chronic or age-related medical condition. Also, it has been observed that while "the rate of older adults with depressive symptoms tends to increase with age, depression is not a normal part of growing older. Rather, in 80% of cases it is a treatable condition" (CDC, 2020). However, not many older people are aware of common symptoms of depression, neither are many aware that they can do a lot on their own to significantly reduce their risk of being depressed. As a result, this chapter is dedicated to issues of mental wellbeing and how older people can live longer, healthier, and happier by paying attention to their emotional needs.

UNDERSTANDING EMOTIONAL NEEDS

The first thing you need to know when it comes to your emotional needs is that they matter. Your emotional needs are just as crucial as any other need you may have to function properly. If you do not pay enough attention to your emotions, they can make you miserable to yourself and the people around you. This is why it is very important for older adults to prioritize creating the right environment for themselves as they grow older. One the basic things you need to take care of for your emotional wellbeing is your environment. If your environment does not offer a strong sense of safety and security, it can be difficult to feel reassured in it and even in your own skin. In the same way, you will want to surround yourself with love, compassion, and positivity. When thinking of love and positivity, the first person you should think of is yourself. Many times older people do not consider the impact of their own thoughts and actions about themselves on their mental health and overall wellbeing. If you allow negative thoughts and negative self-talk to take over your thoughts, you will find it difficult to feel love or express positive affirmations.

Generally, understanding your emotional needs helps to create an anchor of peace within you and give you a sense of reassurance that all is well and will continue to be well. When you have a clear understanding of what your emotional needs are, meeting them will become a fairly simple goal to meet. When thinking of your emotional needs, think of them as the things you need to function properly. According to Schwegman (2021), the common words used by experts to describe your needs are: "validation and acceptance, connection and closeness, safety and security, reassurance, comfort and rest, understanding, attention, fairness, meaning, to matter and feel significant, as well as autonomy and freedom." At different points in your life, you will find that you need any of these things at varying levels. However, before you can progressively have these needs met, there are a few things you will want to do or figure out. Usually, your anxiety increases when you begin to have doubts about who you are or what your purpose is in life. Anxiety can also worsen when you begin to sense fear out of the mixed emotions you may be feeling inside. This anxiety can give rise to other issues that can affect you mentally, including frustration, pessimism, sleep disorders, and depression. Ultimately, this pattern creates a feeling of lacking something and needing something. To avoid this hell hole, ask yourself if you are taking care of yourself the way you should. Ask if your environment is as loving, safe, and reassuring as you would like it to. According to Schwegman (2021),

> When you are having a strong reaction—think fear, anger, anxiety, or desperation, stop and ask yourself, "what am I needing here?" Dive beneath those surface emotions and strong reactions at what lurks beneath them. I often have clients imagine an iceberg. The part of the iceberg that is sticking out of the ocean and can be seen easily are those strong reactions and emotions. But underneath the water and what is harder to see, are those primary fears, needs, and emotions that drive those strong reactions and emotions.

Basically, your emotional needs are usually signs that something is not right and needs to be fixed. For example, consider if you actually have the support system you need around you to function optimally. Everyone needs a support system, so if you are thinking you don't, you should avoid the voice saying that to you as the voice does not love you. Your support system provides an additional backbone for you to rely on and share your worries and anxieties. In times of uncertainties about your identity, your support system can give you the reassurances you need to help you find your courage. Without that support system, you will easily feel lonely, abandoned, or hopeless. Relying on your support system is a sign of strength, not weakness. It is unhealthy to think that as an older adult, you can meet your emotional needs alone without constantly reaching out for support from your loved ones. According to Schwegman (2021),

> One common, unhealthy strategy is by glorifying being a "low-needs, low-maintenance" person. Being go-with-the-flow, flexible, and easy-breezy is encouraged in our culture. We believe the myth that needing is a burden and not needing makes us more lovable. We need to break the belief that it's weak to have needs. So often we starve our needs to the point where we don't even know what we need anymore and can't even name them. I challenge you to let go of the idol of self-sufficiency and lean into connection and vulnerability.

This does not mean you will be totally dependent on other people. Rather, it will be one of your ways of coping with the adverse effects of getting old, which includes an intense feeling of loneliness or isolation. Many times, when you feel isolated, it is probably just in your head. In fact, it is likely that you are the one shutting out everyone else, but you are not seeing it. Also, ask yourself if you are getting enough time to relax and have fun. If you do not have fun regularly, you will experience burnout frequently and blame everyone else but yourself for all your shortcomings or negative feelings and reactions. Playing can also help you fulfil an emotional need that probably arises out of a nostalgic wish to feel things of old or from your youthful past again. Your daily routine will become tiring and frustrating if you do not include periods of resting and having fun in-between. When you create time for fun, you reduce your risk of getting frustrated, pessimistic, lonely, and depressed.

TECHNIQUES FOR STRESS REDUCTION

If your emotional needs increase your desire for peace, safety, and happiness, being stressed will significantly reduce your chances of finding them. Stress has a way of altering our lives and making everything appear worthless. Anyone can be stressed, but the moment you cross the age of 50, the intensity at which you feel stressed can become severe with varying triggers every now and then. If emotional needs make you frustrated and unsociable, stress can make you irritable and toxic. This is not to say stress is a horrible thing you should never want to feel; if you try to do that, you will quickly realize that you actually feel more stressed. Rather, think of stress as a reminder that you need to take a break and recharge. In fact, the American Medical Association has reported that "t more than 80 percent of all diseases are due to stress and strain that originate in the mind and reflect on the boy.(Vital Stream, 2023). Asaa matter of fact, t stress can cause your heart rate and blood flow to increase because of the way it pumps adrenaline throughout your body, causing you to indulge in unhealthy habits that can lead to heart problem.

Stress can also cause you to feel sick and make you more vulnerable to age-related diseases. If you have an existing health condition, stress can make it worse. Some experts believe older people are more likely to deal with stress better. However, stress is still a serious concern for older people, and this is "due in large part to more chronic forms of stress, and the ongoing drumbeat of health concerns, the pressures of caring for ailing relatives, and the increased anxiety around living on a 'fixed' income" (Broudy, 2023). According to Parkview (2021), "Warning signs of stress could include frequent headaches, sleep problems, insomnia, fatigue (physical and mental), difficulty concentrating, change in appetite, muscle tension, pain, chest pain, stomach upset and more." However, anything that makes you more vulnerable to long-term health problems should be avoided. Whether it is a personal or family-related issue that is causing you to feel stressed, the best thing to do is practice stress management techniques to avoid more damage in the long run.

One of the first things you want to do when you start feeling stressed or when you notice any of the symptoms mentioned in this book is shut yourself off from anything that looks like or sound like a trigger or stressor. It might be something as common as accumulated medical costs or a family emergency that is already being taken care of by someone in the family. Because older people have a tendency to worry about everything, you may find that you are feeling stressed about these developments. So, shut yourself off and think about any lazy thing you enjoy doing, whether watching a comic movie or listening to your favorite songs, and say to yourself as many times as you want "all is well." By assuring yourself that all is well, you are transmitting a message that is contrary to stress to your brain and registering a more positive note throughout your body.

In addition, you can take a short walk of 5 to 10 minutes and just feel the natural air around you and remind yourself again that all will be well. You can also talk to a friend, try light exercises, or do a little body stretching to reduce the anxiety in your body system. If you feel like it might help, try to get a lapdog or any pet of your choice. Apart from these, you can also get in touch with your doctor or health provider and talk about how you feel. They should be able to recommend something that can help you relax more and feel less anxious. In fact, experts recommend different techniques to older people to help them destress, from medications to sleep and yoga therapy. On your own, or with the help of a specialist, you can practice sleep therapy, massage therapy, sound therapy, drawing, or anything else that feel like fun to you. You can even get on the internet and watch funny videos.

MINDFULNESS AND GRATITUDE

Mindfulness and gratitude are important ingredients of the aging process. Mindfulness helps to deepen your self-awareness and self-healing abilities while gratitude enhances the quality of your life. When you think of mindfulness, think of it as the key to living fully in the present, of being aware of who you are, and of making the best out of your senior years. According to Tallon (2020),

> Mindfulness is the ability to stay in the present moment and to focus your thoughts on what is happening in the here and now. It's our ability to not think about the past or the future but to instead observe what is happening in the moment.

Why does mindfulness matter for older adults? Well, for one, it helps to improve your cognitive abilities, your level of productivity, and your ability to function at full your full capacity. You can also practice mindfulness to enhance your ability to focus better in any given situation. We live in a world full of distractions; from our daily experiences with our families and friends to the ways in which activities in the outside world can affect our environment and mood. If you begin to think of mindfulness as the way you try to anchor yourself and stay grounded in spite of the distractions, you will find that it is a really helpful process. Also, mindfulness is a good antidote for overcoming stress and mood disorders.

As older adults, practicing mindfulness helps to ensure a balance between your emotions and actions. Mindfulness practice is about resolving any type of chaos you may feel inside you through self-evaluation and self-love. It is also about learning to not be too critical of yourself and learning to forgive yourself for the things you may not be very proud of. One of the most helpful ways you can practice mindfulness is by avoid judging yourself. Even as seniors who have seen a lot in life, there are things that you will do sometimes that may seem disappointing to you. You may be harsh on yourself as a result, thinking you should know not to do that much at your age. But the fact that you already acknowledged your wrong is a sign of growth, so you should not be so harsh on yourself to the point that it makes you feel sad and depressed. This is another vital reason why you should practice mindfulness: it is about engaging your mind to understand what is eating at your inner peace. Through mindfulness, you can improve the quality of your sleep and thoughts, the impact of your actions, the quality of your social life and relationships, as well as the your mental and overall health. Mindfulness enhances self-growth and happiness, and the more you practice it, the more your happiness and sense of fulfilment will increase. In fact, mindfulness has been proven to also reduce severe pain, whether physical or emotional (Tallon, 2020).

Another crucial advantage of mindfulness is that it provides clarity. As we grow older, the quality of our cognitive process will likely experience some level of decline, and our ability to make quality decisions can be affected a little. However, the more we exercise the mind, the more likely it is that we can slow down the cognitive impairment that is associated with the aging process. The human mind is a really powerful organ, and the more engaged it is, the more resilient it will likely be. Also, the lovely thing about mindfulness is that you can do it anywhere and at anytime. Since mindfulness is about being present and engaging the mind to find inner peace and establish a sense of clarity, the most important ingredient you need is your willingness to practice it.

So, how can you practice mindfulness? Well, according to Tallon (2020), you can try centering exercises; do some breathing exercises; eat mindfully; "fire up your five senses"; and appreciate and interact more with nature. You can also practice mindfulness through a deliberate routine strategy that helps you maximze productivity and self-awareness. For example, you can decide to practice mindfulness for 10 to 15 minutes when you wake up in the morning. You can also do another 10 to 15 minutes after lunch, and another 10 to 15 minutes before you sleep at night. After each mindfulness exercise, the process, take note of how you felt and what it tells you about the process you just went through. As you practice more and more, you will begin to get into it easily and use different mindfulness techniques to enhance your experiences each and every day.

Basically, if you approach any activity on mindfulness with the mindset that you only have to be fully present, you will be able to maximize the benefits of the process. Whether you are walking, standing, dancing, eating, drinking, journaling, or meditating in silence, the more you can put your entire self into the process and approach your thoughts and feelings without any judgement, the more you will be able to enjoy the full benefits of mindfulness. This is not an easy thing to do in any way, especially if you are trying it for the first time. However, it gets better the more you practice.

Another way to practice mindfulness is through gratitude. In so many ways, gratitude can change your view of yourself and the world very quickly. If you find that you are growing pessimistic about things every day, try practicing gratitude. For example, writing out the things you are grateful for can make a gigantic difference in the quality of your thoughts. The point of any activity on gratitude is to show you that even when things look very bad, there is always another angle from which you can look at things and feel better. In this regard, Robert Emmons has observed that there are two ways to think about gratitude (Millacci, 2017):

First comes the acknowledgment of goodness in one's life. In a state of gratitude, we say yes to life. We affirm that, all in all, life is good and has elements that make it worth living. The acknowledgment that we have received something gratifies us, both by its presence and by the effort the giver put into choosing it.

Second, gratitude is recognizing that sources of this goodness lie outside the self. One can be grateful to our creator, other people, animals, and the world, but not to oneself. At this stage, we recognize the goodness in our lives and who to thank for it.

Essentially, when you practice gratitude, you are expressing thankfulness for the things you know and don't know are working in your favor. Gratitude has a way of positively impacting your sleep pattern, mental and overall health, as well as your self-esteem and spiritual life. By practicing gratitude, you are training yourself to see the silver lining in any bad situation, and the good surrounding your life because you are alive. According to the famous Buddhist and meditation expert, Jack Kornfield, "Being grateful for not only life's blessing but also its suffering is a key component of living a spiritual life—and more broadly, to a fulfilling and meaningful life" (Gregoire, 2014). Gratitude teaches you to appreciate the gift of life, and the blessings of your relationships.

There are many things you can be grateful for and many ways to practice gratitude. You can make gratitude into a personal ritual by choosing to write two things that you are grateful for every day you wake up to a new day. Start by getting yourself a gratitude journal and only use it for practicing gratitude. Whenever you are feeling down, you can always open the journal and read out the things you wrote aloud. If it happens that you feel different about those things you had written before, take your time to ask why and practice mindfulness to truly understand. Also, you can practice gratitude with family and friends to increase the quality of your social connectedness. The more time you put into practicing, the better you will get at it.

PROFESSIONAL HELP AND SUPPORT

When it comes to your emotional wellbeing, do not ever think that you have to do it by yourself. Despite the mindfulness and gratitude techniques in this chapter, you might still find sometimes that you are not in a great place mentally. This is nothing to be ashamed about, and it is the reason there are now more than a few professional help resources for everyone, particularly for older adults. Know that you are not alone. For example, the Centers for Disease Control and Prevention (CDC) has revealed that

> upwards of 59% of Americans will be diagnosed with a mental illness at some point in their lifetime. One in five Americans will experience a mental illness within a year. And, one out of every 25 Americans lives with a serious mental illness (major depression, bipolar disorder, and schizophrenia, as examples). (Debolt, 2020)

At the same time, when George Jerjian, a mindset coach who found his way out of post-retirement depression, conducted a survey that involved over 15,000 retirees who were 60 and older, he found that identity, health, and regret were cited by the participants as their "single biggest challenge in retirement" (Jerjian, 2022). In the same way, when Nora Super, 59, shared the story of her struggle with depression with other people, she said: "In disclosing my illness to others, I've discovered that most people I know have been touched by mental illness in some way" (Super, 2021). If there is anything to learn from these stories, it is that many older people go through one type of mental health problem or another at some point in their later years. You are not alone if you also feel this way. Also, you should seek the help of a professional if your sleep quality has worsened, or if you are overindulging in any type of substance, or if you are constantly feeling tired, anxious, unmotivated, sad, or depressed. At no point should you allow yourself to feel ashamed to ask for help, or to think that no one will listen to you, or that you are all alone and isolated from all the good in the world. This thought pattern is a sign that you need to speak to mental health professional.

As older adults, the first person you should speak to when seeking professional help is your personal doctor. They know your medical history and are in the best position to recommend a professional who can help you. For example, it has been observed that "people with depression have a higher risk of developing stroke, type 2 diabetes, and heart disease. And, this can also occur in reverse—people with certain chronic health conditions can be more susceptible to developing mental illness" (Debolt, 2020). So, by keeping your doctor in the loop, they can also monitor your progress and make appropriate recommendations that might help you feel better quickly. In the end, the person who stands to benefit the most from this process is you. By taking your mental health seriously, you are practically increasing your chances of living a longer, healthier, and happier life.

CHAPTER 7

THE GOLDEN BALANCE-A LIFE OF FULFILLMENT AND CONNECTION

"Happiness is not a matter of intensity but of balance,
order, rhythm and harmony."
– Thomas Merton

At the end of the day, the greatest gift anyone can hope to have is to live every day feeling fulfilled, healthy, and surrounded by love, compassion, and support. These elements are usually associated with a life that is shaped by great level of balance. Older adults experience more balance in old age when they are able to enjoy mental, financial, social, and health stability. When put together, you will find that your sense of happiness, satisfaction, and fulfillment will improve significantly. However, as we have shown so far in this book, it takes work and personal commitment to excellence to achieve balance. For example, if you were to rate your life's balance now between 1 and 10, what would be your answer? Now, you should know that anything below 5 means there is still a lot of work to be done. Between 6 and 8 means there is room for improvement, and 9 or 10 means you have to keep up the great work you are already doing.

Generally, living a balanced life does not mean everything is rosy and perfect. If anything, it means you have been able to perfect the art of management, of making sure that one side of your life does not outweigh the other in a way that puts you at a disadvantage. As Thomas Merton has explained, a life of balance is a life in order, with as little avoidable chaos as possible, and with a strong personal commitment to keeping things balanced. If you can imagine life in old age as a quest for balance, finding purpose and fulfillment, and developing a stronger connection with yourself and the people you love, you will find that your overall wellbeing will be in top shape and you will enjoy a high level of happiness. At the same time, achieving balance is a process, and many times the road can be tougher than imagined, especially when there are unexpected bumps on the way. These bumps might be things about your health, financial situation, emotional state, family troubles, and so on. If care is not taken, unexpected bumps in life can derail a person's journey to finding balance. But I hope the resources in this chapter will prove helpful for you.

Why Balance Matters

Have you ever wondered how it is that some people seem to always have their affairs in order and others just don't? The reason why this is so is mostly because it takes planning, intentionality, and a sense of responsibility to have your affairs together. For example, if you want to increase your chances of staying healthy and alive past the 100-year mark, you have to decide to live a more healthy life. This requires that you stay away from substance abuse of any type, avoid or significantly reduce your consumption of alcohol, drink enough water, get enough sleep (about 9 hours every night), reduce your stress levels, abide by your coping mechanisms for emotional distress, go for your check-ups as often as you have to, develop a strong support system and maintain a good social connectedness, and so on. Also, make sure that you are dedicating enough time to self-care. Sometimes, all you need to feel like everything is where they should be is a little appreciation of your body. Always pay attention to your looks and surroundings. Even if your personal hygiene is good, if your environment is not hygienic, you are likely to still feel squeamish, not just because you want to but mainly because your body takes note. Your body absorbs everything, so the cleaner your environment, the more likely it is that your mood will improve. Also, from time to time, do something you really enjoy doing. Appreciate life and the fact that you are able to live in it. These are all basic measure you can take to maintain balance in your life. When you start taking measures to ensure balance in your life, it might seem like an unnecessary chore. But as time goes on, you will find that your life is easier and better for it.

One of the reasons why balance is crucial is that it helps you develop resilient strategies when things begin to get shaky. The moment things begin to go off, say maybe you stop getting enough sleep all of a sudden, or your stress levels begin to rise dramatically, that is a good sign that you need to take a break on any activity or situation that is starting to make a hell out of your life. If you feel like you have been taking on too many things, then it's time to cut back. If you feel like your family or social situation is beginning to overwhelm you, then it's time to take a step back. Proritize your mental and physical health over getting along with people who do not prioritize your wellbeing. Let the number of yeses you you say to people be within your threshold of tolerance. At no point should you try to force yourself through emotionally or physically distressful situations. If you are feeling more and more frustrated or find that you are getting easily upset, know that it is time to check in with yourself and see where imbalance may be happening. Also, if you find that you are suddenly not feeling happy or satisfied with your life ask yourself if anything has changed and if you have been practicing gratitude as you should. Sometimes, it can be the smallest things that will shake you to your roots and make you feel as if your life is in complete disorder. Do not allow the negative thoughts to win. Remember that as older adults, your tolerance level is not the same as it was in your youth, and your body and mind are practically on the verge of breaking down if you let too many stressors invade those spaces.

At the same time, your quest for balance should not overshadow your ability to be compassionate and empathetic. In fact, there may times when you cannot avoid going out of your way for a friend or family member, but be sure that those are one of the extraordinary moments that you can't miss. For example, if any of your children or grandchildren are getting married, or if your friend is celebrating a landmark event, or any other situation that might fall within that category. The secret to enjoying a life of balance is in knowing when to say yes and when to say no. As older adults, the first person you should be least willing to overstretch is yourselves. The human body takes note of everything, but the older adult's body takes note faster than anyone else. When making decisions about what to say yes or no to, ask yourself what will happen if you say no and ask what will happen if you say yes. You can write out your answers. Any time the number of things on one side of the divide outnumber the other side, then you know you have your answer. It does not happen often, but if there is ever a tie, then you can either choose to do nothing or ask yourself what will happen if you do nothing. If your opinion is not enough, ask a family member or friend to weigh in on the situation. The more you repeat this exercise, the more you will realize the significance of making the right decisions for the sake of balance.

In addition, keep in mind that there will always be times when your ability to maintain balance in your life will be tested. Say, for example, the COVID-19 pandemic. It is no exaggeration to say everything that could possibly go wrong went wrong during the pandemic. Apart from the fact that older adults were more susceptible to the disease than the rest of the population, everyone was required to abide by the social isolation rules and struggle with the many uncertainties caused by the pandemic. Senior community groups and social support systems were practically shut down and all you had was yourself and sometimes your family. Extreme situations like that can test your balance, and no one would blame you if you find yourself falling a level or two below on the balance scale. However, extreme situations like that can be the type of training you need to build your resilience and significantly improve your standing on the balance scale. But this requires having a strong can-do spirit and never giving in when faced with adversity. It also requires a solid commitment to constant practice, making sure every step of the way that your actions are serving a greater purpose of keeping the balance in your life. This kind of spirit can make it a lot easier to cope with extreme life circumstances that might send other people bumping along the bottom on the balance scale.

TO A WELL-ROUNDED LIFE

For the most part, everything you need to maintain a well-rounded life in old age has been mentioned in this book. According to Good (2023), "What is considered balance for one is not considered balance for all. But one thing is true, our success as creators of a balanced lifestyle is based on mind over matter." This is simply the foundation you need for living a truly well-rounded life. The key is to master the difference between when to take a step back and when to push ahead. Also, maintaining a well-rounded life requires that you always let your knowledge of your strengths and weaknesses guide your actions. This is because older adults are not the same across the board. While some people have never had any serious health complication all their lives, there are those who have had to deal with one health problem or the other. In the same way, there are older adults who will never have to struggle about anything for the remainder of their lives. The comfortable life situation of those seniors cannot be compared to other seniors who still have to work a job out of necessity at 70 years or older. This does not mean that the seniors who go to work have a miserable life; it simply means that circumstances are different. But this does not mean they cannot have a well-rounded life. The important question any older adult should always ask is: how well am I balancing my life? Am I getting enough rest? Am I taking enough time to meditate and practice mindfulness? Am I maintaining a positive social life? What am I doing right or wrong at this stage in my life? These are all examples of question any older adult can ask to check in with themself, regardless of their circumstances.

Further, let your actions be guided by genuine self-love. At the end of the day, no one can make you love yourself. If you love yourself enough, you will always put your health, safety, and happiness first. This is especially important when you are trying to live a well-rounded life. Be sure that your commitment to the well-rounded life is not half-hearted. For example, you should not substitute one unhealthy habit for another. If you decide to quit smoking because of the many health hazards associated with it, do not then switch to excess alcohol consumption as your way of "making up" for the fun you may think you have been missing out on since you decided to quit smoking. There are many other ways you can spice up your fun life without putting your health in danger. Equally, maintaining a well-rounded life is also about paying attention to every slight changes in your body. If you feel the urge to indulge certain bodily needs, discuss first with your doctor to know your limits. Also, if you start noticing any unusual signs that your health might be in danger, do not ignore the signs. Having a balanced life requires that you build a good relationship with your doctor in case of emergencies or any random health concern you might have.

EMBRACING CHANGES AND TRANSITIONS

Whether we like it or not, we all are part of a natural process that started the day we were born. The aging process is an unavoidable process for all of us, and understanding that this is our reality makes it easier for us to navigate our world in relation to older adults. Usually, the average human being begins to notice natural changes in the color of their hair and the texture of their skin from middle age (Amarya *et al.*, 2018). As we grow older, our vulnerability to stroke, Alzheimer's disease, Parkinson's disease, and other age-related diseases will increase (Amarya *et al.*, 2018). Because of the age-related changes that we all experience, the aging process can significantly affect our memory. As a matter of fact, research has shown that "The whole group of changes taking place in the brain with ageing decreases the efficiency of cell-to-cell communication, which declines the ability to retrieve and learn" (Amarya *et al.*, 2018). In addition, all our five senses and their capacities to function optimally are affected by the aging process, and our bodies undergo transitions in size that can vary from one person to another. For example, in the United States, older adults between the ages of 60 and 79 years old are at a higher risk of becoming obese, with men estimated to have a 38.1% obesity risk and women a 42.5% obesity risk (Amarya *et al.*, 2018). In the United Kingdom, 12% of older men from 75 years and above are at risk of obesity while 22% of older women within the same age bracket are at risk of obesity (Amarya *et al.*, 2018). In short, there are certain age-related changes that are unavoidable for all of us, particularly for some older adults. While it is not all older adults that get diagnosed with Parkinson's disease, all older adults are vulnerable to higher stress levels and changes in their physical and mental health.

At the same time, vulnerability is not the same as inescapable certainty. This is why it is crucial to embrace age-related changes and transitions early. Although acknowledging these changes matter, how you transition from one phase of age-related change to another matters more. Major life transitions force us to question everything about who we are and what we want out of life. How you manage transitions can determine the potential effects the changes you undergo will have on you. Experts have recommended various ways you can successfully manage a transition from one stage of life to another. According to Joelson (2017), you will likely "Experience a range of negative feelings (anger, anxiety, confusion, numbness, and self-doubt)" at the beginning of your transition. Additionally, Joelson (2017) believes you will "Feel a loss of self-esteem" before you start to come to terms with the changes that made the transition necessary. After this, you will begin to "Acknowledge that you need to let go of the past and accept the future," before allowing yourself to "feel hopeful about the future" (Joelson, 2017). Subsequently, you will experience an uptick in your self-esteem and "develop an optimistic view of the future" (Joelson, 2017). These stages of transition do not only happen when you become older. According to Hayles (2020), you can also experience major life transitions when you lose a job, change your career, get married, have children, experience empty nest syndrome, experience serious health problems, lose someone that is very close to you, and when you retire.

In this case, however, the best thing to do is to let the stages of your transition play out one after the other. Do not rush through it and do not ignore your healing process. If you allow the stages of transition to play out as they should, you will come out of the process a better, stronger, and healthier human being. Also, you can rely on your support system such as your family and close friends to help you through those difficult periods. But do not forget that there may also be times when the only real support system you will have is yourself and probably a therapist. For example, you may have experienced a loss of close friends or family members, and in your time of grief you may not have the usual people around to run to anymore. Another good example is the story of 74-year-old Bruce Cowper, who was married twice before but has been living as a divorcé for more than 10 years. Cowper is of the opinion that healing and completion comes from within, and after coming to this realization, he said: "I was barking up the wrong tree. If I wanted to feel content and complete, it had to come from within me, rather than looking for it out there somewhere, or in someone else" (Vinall, 2021). Like Cowper, 72-year-old Di Moloney and 70-year-old Kerrie Lorimer, whose separate marriages have been over for decades, believe they are happier and more independent women despite being alone (Vinall, 2021).

Meanwhile, you may find that you are not as independent as these older people, and that is also fine. You can seek the help of an external voice, like a mental health specialist, to help you through difficult transition periods. For example, 69-year-old Marian Elliott was divorced at the age of 60 by her husband whom she married at 22 years old. Her pain was severe when he left, and she thought "a marriage broken up by the other person is like a bereavement", particularly because she had imagined she would spend the rest of her life with her ex-husband (Cocozza, 2022). However, after he left, she signed up for conselling with a specialist who also helped her deal with the grief of losing her father who died when she was 20, which she had not processed (Cocozza, 2022). After a while, she joined a local organization because, as she said: "I knew I needed people" (Cocozza, 2022). Now, she is enjoying a life of freedom, happiness, and fulfillment with the constant support of her friends through whom she has learned that "there is still lots for me to enjoy and do. They have enabled me, through their friendliness, to make a new life all by myself. And that's quite an empowering feeling" (Cocozza, 2022).

Essentially, you get to decide how you want to go about your transition in the aging process, whether alone or with the help of professionals and friends. As you begin to heal and embrace the changes that come with the aging process, learn to also live in the moment and practice breathing exercises from time to time. That you are the one alive now does not mean you will always be, which should serve as a good reason to practice gratitude and take your healing and happiness seriously.

CONCLUSION

In writing this book, I have tried to show that you can live a happy and fulfilling life without giving in to loneliness and social isolation. One of the biggest regrets that older people have later in life is the feeling of wishing they had lived more, that they had gone out and met more people, or that they had more love, empathy, and compassion. Let the new social skills you have learned in this book guide your interactions with the people you will be meeting and associating with from now. Living more is all about embracing the aging process and all its advantages and disadvantages. I hope that you will use what you know now to live a happier and more independent life.

Remember that getting old is not the end of the world; it is the beginning of a new chapter in your beautiful story. In all that you do, always put your health, safety, and happiness first. Prioritize your self-care and regular check-ups, and don't forget to practice gratitude, mindfulness, and meditation. Go out more and enjoy the beauty of nature with family and friends. Spend time developing old connections and building new ones. Also, never forget that it is never too late to start something new, and it is never too late to have fun. Focus more on your mental and physical health, and stay away from unhealthy habits that can shorten your life expectancy.

You are not missing out on life, you are actually enjoying the view from a different angle, and it is probably the best view in all the world. You are an awesome person, and the world is better because you are in it. Life is wonderful; do not let anything weigh you down for long. Even when you are alone, there is so much you can give to yourself and the world. The world is waiting to be blessed by you, and I hope you will be willing, now or sooner, to spread your awesomeness throughout its length and breadth.

CHAPTER
"GOOD WILL"

Helping others without expectation of anything in return has been proven to lead to increased happiness and satisfaction in life.

I would love to give you the chance to experience that same feeling during your reading or listening experience today…

All it takes is a few moments of your time to answer one simple question:

<u>Would you make a difference in the life of someone you've never met—without spending any money or seeking recognition for your good will?</u>

If so, I have a small request for you.

If you've found value in your reading or listening experience today, I humbly ask that you take a brief moment right now to leave an honest review of this book. It won't cost you anything but 30 seconds of your time—just a few seconds to share your thoughts with others.

Your voice can go a long way in helping someone else find the same inspiration and knowledge that you have.

Are you familiar with leaving a review for an Audible, Kindle, or e-reader book? If so, it's simple:

If you're on **Audible**: just hit the three dots in the top right of your device, click rate & review, then leave a few sentences about the book along with your star rating.

If you're reading on **Kindle** or an e-reader, simply scroll to the last page of the book and swipe up—the review should prompt from there.

If you're on a **Paperback** or any other physical format of this book, you can find the book page on Amazon (or wherever you bought this) and leave your review right there.

REFERENCES

Ackerman, C. (2017, December 18). *87 self-reflection questions for introspection*. PositivePsychology. https://positivepsychology.com/introspection-self-reflection/

Amarya, S., Singh, K., & Sabharwal, M. (2018). Ageing process and physiological changes. In *www.intechopen.com*. IntechOpen. https://www.intechopen.com/chapters/60564

ASC. (2014, March 23). *The importance of exercise for seniors*. American Senior Communities (ASC). https://www.asccare.com/importance-exercise-seniors/

AshaRani, P., Lai, D., Koh, J., & Subramaniam, M. (2022). Purpose in life in older adults: A systematic review on conceptualization, measures, and determinants. *International Journal of Environmental Research and Public Health, 19*(10), 5860. https://doi.org/10.3390/ijerph19105860

Betchen, S. J. (2020, October 9). *The Importance of shared interests in relationships*. Psychology Today. https://www.psychologytoday.com/intl/blog/magnetic-partners/202010/the-importance-shared-interests-in-relationships

Broudy, O. (2023, June 27). *What stress does to the body after 50*. AARP. https://www.aarp.org/health/healthy-living/info-2023/how-stress-affects-your-health-after-50.html

C. S. Lewis Quotes. (n.d.). *Quotes*. Www.quotes.net. Retrieved September 7, 2023, from https://www.quotes.net/quote/37151

Centers for Disease Control and Prevention (CDC). (2020, August 21). *State of mental health and aging in America (MAHA)*. Www.cdc.gov. https://www.cdc.gov/aging/publications/ mental-health.html

Centers for Disease Control and Prevention (CDC). (2021, February 17). *How much physical activity do older adults need?* Www.cdc.gov. https://www.cdc.gov/physicalactivity/ba- sics/older_adults/index.htm#:~:text=As%20an%20older%20 adult%2C%20regular

Cherry, K. (2021, September 1). *The health consequences of loneliness.* Verywell Mind. https://www.verywellmind.com/ loneliness-causes-effects-and-treatments-2795749

Cocozza, P. (2022, May 16). A new start after 60: "Alone for the first time in my life, I learned how to be happy." *The Guardian.* https://www.theguardian.com/lifeandstyle/2022/ may/16/a-new-start-after-60-alone-for-the-first-time-in- my-life-i-learned-how-to-be-happy

Cocuzzo, B., Wrench, A., & O'Malley, C. (2022). Effects of COVID-19 on older adults: Physical, mental, emotional, so- cial, and financial problems seen and unseen. *Cureus, 14*(9). https://doi.org/10.7759/cureus.29493

Colino, S. (2020, October). *How loneliness affects health.* Brain- andLife. https://www.brainandlife.org/articles/how-loneli- ness-affects-health

Cuncic, A. (2022, November 9). *What is active listening?* Very- well Mind. https://www.verywellmind.com/what-is-ac- tive-listening-3024343

Debolt, C. (2020, December 17). *Top barriers to mental health treatment.* Futures Recovery. https://futuresrecoveryhealth- care.com/blog/barriers-to-mental-health-treatment/#:~:- text=challenges%20the%20most.-

Desilva, D., & Anderson-Villaluz, D. (2021, July 20). *Nutrition as we age: Healthy eating with the dietary guidelines.* Health.gov. https://health.gov/news/202107/nutrition-we-age-healthy-eating-dietary-guidelines#:~:text=Older%20adults%20generally%20have%20lower

Dykstra, P. A. (2009). Older adult loneliness: myths and realities. *European Journal of Ageing, 6*(2), 91–100. https://doi.org/10.1007/s10433-009-0110-3

Eure, M. A. (2023, June 21). *Why yearly checkups for seniors are key.* Verywell Health. https://www.verywellhealth.com/your-annual-checkup-2966782

Firman, T. (2019, May 2). *50 questions you should always ask your doctor after 50.* Best Life. https://bestlifeonline.com/doctor-questions-after-50/

Fitting Fitness In. (2021, January 28). *Success story: Meet 2 "older" superwomen who prove the power of fitness.* Fitting Fitness In. https://www.fittingfitnessin.com/2021/01/success-story-meet-2-older-superwomen-who-prove-the-power-of-fitness/

Garis, M. G. (2020, November 12). *Loneliness and being alone aren't the same thing.* Well+Good. https://www.wellandgood.com/difference-between-being-alone-being-lonely/

Gil-Lacruz, M., Saz-Gil, M. I., & Gil-Lacruz, A. I. (2019). Benefits of Older Volunteering on Wellbeing: An International Comparison. *Frontiers in Psychology, 10.* https://doi.org/10.3389/fpsyg.2019.02647

Gillet, R., & Feloni, R. (2017, November 29). *19 extremely successful people who changed careers after turning 30.* Inc. https://www.inc.com/business-insider/people-who-found-success-and-changed-careers-after-30-years-old.html#:~:text=Martha%20Stewart%20was%20a%20full,now%20Martha%20Stewart%20Living%20Omnimedia.

Good, S. "Honey. (2023, July 4). *How to find mental balance in your life after 60.* Sixty and Me. https://sixtyandme.com/how-to-find-mental-balance-in-your-life-after-60/

Goodreads. (n.d.). *A quote by Ralph Waldo Emerson.* Www. goodreads.com. Retrieved September 8, 2023, from https://www.goodreads.com/quotes/64541-the-purpose-of-life-is-not-to-be-happy-it

Gregoire , C. (2014, May 19). *Jack Kornfield on gratitude and mindfulness.* Greater Good. https://greatergood.berkeley.edu/article/item/jack_kornfield_on_gratitude_and_mindfulness

Habash, C. (2022, February 1). *What is self-reflection, and why is it important for self-improvement?* Thriveworks. https://thriveworks.com/blog/importance-self-reflection-improvement/

Hartwell-Walker, M. (2019, August 4). *The importance of celebrating milestones together.* Psych Central. https://psychcentral.com/blog/the-importance-of-celebrating-milestones-together#2

Haslam, A. (2018, August 14). *How to create your own safe space at home.* Thrive Global. https://community.thriveglobal.com/how-to-create-your-own-safe-space-at-home/

Hayles, R. (2020, June 7). *Life transitions: 8 tips for getting through tough times.* Summit Family Therapy. https://summitfamilytherapy.com/summit-family-therapy-peoria-illinois-blog/2020/6/7/life-transitions-8-tips-for-getting-through-tough-times

Homewatch CareGivers. (2022, May 25). *10 healthy meals for seniors that are quick and easy to make.* Homewatch CareGivers. https://www.homewatchcaregivers.com/blog/health-tips/10-healthy-meals-for-seniors-that-are-quick-and-/

Jerjian, G. (2022). Inside a retiree's $420/month apartment by the beach in Mexico. In *CNBC.* https://www.cnbc.com/2022/06/15/67-year-old-who-unretired-at-62-shares-

the-biggest-retirement-challenge-that-no-one-talks-about.
html

Jim Rohn Quotes. (n.d.). BrainyQuote. Retrieved September 10, 2023, from https://www.brainyquote.com/quotes/
jim_rohn_147499

Joelson, R. B. (2017, July 9). *Managing difficult life transitions.*
Richard B. Joelson, DSW. https://richardbjoelsondsw.com/
articles/managing-difficult-life-transitions/

Killam, K. (2020, August 6). *5 Major Myths About Loneliness
| Psychology Today.* Psychology Today. https://www.psychologytoday.com/us/blog/social-health/202008/5-major-myths
about-loneliness

Kilroy, D. S. (2014, September 8). *Exercise plan for seniors:
Strength, stretching, and balance.* Healthline. https://www.healthline.com/health/everyday-fitness/senior-workouts#minute-strength-routine

Lagemann, J. (2022, September 30). *11 meaningful ways older adults can volunteer right now.* Forbes Health. https://www.
forbes.com/health/healthy-aging/volunteer-opportunities-for-older-adults/

Lane, A. B. (2021, April 1). *Research shows that volunteering
makes us happier.* Community Tech Network (CTN). https://
communitytechnetwork.org/blog/research-shows-that-volunteering-makes-us-happier/

Langmann, E. (2022). Vulnerability, ageism, and health: is it
helpful to label older adults as a vulnerable group in health
care? *Medicine, Health Care and Philosophy, 26*(1). https://doi.
org/10.1007/s11019-022-10129-5

Laurence Sterne Quotes. (n.d.). BrainyQuote. Retrieved
September 10, 2023, from https://www.brainyquote.com/
quotes/laurence_sterne_155708

Leonard, B., & Kreitzer, M.J. (n.d.). *What is life purpose?* Taking Charge of Your Health & Wellbeing. Retrieved September 8, 2023, from https://www.takingcharge.csh.umn.edu/what-life-purpose#:~:text=Your%20life%20purpose%20consists%20of

Madeson, M. (2023, March 28). *How to overcome loneliness according to psychology.* PositivePsychology.com. https://positive-psychology.com/loneliness-psychology/#google_vignette

McMullen, M. (2021, July 22). *The value of social connectedness for older adults.* Fitbit Health Solutions. https://healthsolutions.fitbit.com/blog/the-value-of-social-connectedness-for-older-adults/#:~:text=Social%20Connectedness%20Improves%20Older%20Adults%27%20Quality%20of%20Life&text=Staying%20socially%20connected%20may%20result

Millacci, T. S. (2017, February 28). *What is gratitude and why is it so important?* Positive Psychology. https://positivepsychology.com/gratitude-appreciation/

Morin, A. (2017, August 5). *7 Science-Backed Reasons You Should Spend More Time Alone.* Forbes. https://www.forbes.com/sites/amymorin/2017/08/05/7-science-backed-reasons-you-should-spend-more-time-alone/?sh=123bd78d-1b7e

Morse, E. (2022, May 5). *Reciprocity in relationships: 3 types of reciprocity.* MasterClass. https://www.masterclass.com/articles/reciprocity-in-relationships

Parkview. (2021, April 26). *Stress and its effect on older adults .* Parkview.com. https://www.parkview.com/blog/stress-and-its-effect-on-older-adults#:~:text=For%20seniors%2C%20stress%20often%20manifests

Raman, R. (2017, September 5). *How your nutritional needs change as you age.* Healthline. https://www.healthline.com/

nutrition/nutritional-needs-and-aging#How-Does-Aging-Affect-Your-Nutritional-Needs?

Robbins, T. (n.d.). *12 tips on finding your purpose in life*. Tony Robbins. Retrieved September 8, 2023, from https://www.tonyrobbins.com/stories/date-with-destiny/what-is-my-purpose/

Schwegman, K., & LCSW. (2021, September 20). *How to identify and get your emotional needs met*. Holistic Wellness Practice. https://www.holisticwellnesspractice.com/hwp-blog/2021/09/20/how-to-identify-and-get-your-emotional-needs-met

Senior Lifestyle. (2020, February 4). *7 best exercises for seniors (and a few to avoid!)*. Senior Lifestyle. https://www.seniorlifestyle.com/resources/blog/7-best-exercises-for-seniors-and-a-few-to-avoid/

Shannon, M. (2020, December 26). *6 technologies seniors can use to keep in touch with loved ones*. CCACC Adult Day Care Center. https://www.ccaccadultdaycare.org/post/6-technologies-seniors-can-use-to-keep-in-touch-with-loved-ones

Shiel, W. C. (2018, October 19). *General medical checkup*. EMedicineHealth; eMedicineHealth. https://www.emedicinehealth.com/checkup/article_em.htm

Subramanian, I. (2020, December 1). *6 myths about social isolation*. BrainandLife. https://www.brainandlife.org/the-magazine/online-exclusives/6-myths-about-social-isolation/

Super, N. (2021). Opening up about my struggle with recurring depression. *Health Affairs, 40*(11), 1806–1810. https://doi.org/10.1377/hlthaff.2021.00894

Tallon, M. (2020, April 13). *10 simple ways to practice mindfulness in our daily life*. Monique Tallon. https://moniquetallon.com/10-simple-ways-to-practice-mindfulness-in-our-daily-life/

Tavel, R. (2021, August 2). *A guide to the best exercises for seniors*. Forbes Health. https://www.forbes.com/health/healthy-aging/best-exercises-for-seniors/

Thomas Merton Quotes. (n.d.). BrainyQuote. Retrieved September 11, 2023, from https://www.brainyquote.com/quotes/thomas_merton_385072

Vengrow, B. (n.d.). *The importance of friends as you age*. Aetna. Retrieved September 7, 2023, from https://www.aetna.com/health-guide/importance-of-friends-as-you-age.html

Villines, Z. (2022, April 28). How to show emotional support: Tips and examples. *Medical News Today*. https://www.medicalnewstoday.com/articles/emotional-support

Vinall, M. (2021, June 5). Gleefully single seniors: "If I wanted to feel complete, it had to come from within." *The Guardian*. https://www.theguardian.com/lifeandstyle/2021/jun/06/gleefully-single-seniors-if-i-wanted-to-feel-complete-it-had-to-come-from-within

Vital Stream. (2023, March 6). *The benefits of massages over the age of 70*. Vital Stream. https://vitalstream.nl/en/the-benefits-of-massages-over-the-age-of-70/

Vogels, E. A. (2019, September 9). *Millennials stand out for their technology use, but older generations also embrace digital life*. Pew Research Center. https://www.pewresearch.org/short-reads/2019/09/09/us-generations-technology-use/

Wilbanks, K. (2017, June 25). *The unsurpassed joy of celebrating milestones with friends*. Kim Wilbanks. https://kimwilbanks.com/2017/06/24/the-unsurpassed-joy-of-celebrating-milestones-with-friends/

William James Quotes. (n.d.). BrainyQuote. Retrieved September 11, 2023, from https://www.brainyquote.com/quotes/william_james_385478

Zaraska, M. (2023, February 28). *How loneliness reshapes the brain.* QuantamaGazine. https://www.quantamagazine.org/how-loneliness-reshapes-the-brain-20230228/#:~:text=Feelings%20of%20loneliness%20prompt%20changes,isolate%20people%20from%20social%20contact.&text=Loneliness%20doesn%27t%20just%20make,trust%20and%20connect%20to%20others.

ABOUT THE AUTHOR

This author has a knack for capturing the essence of life's complexities, intricacies, and universal truths through her writing, often presenting thought-provoking perspectives on various aspects of existence. Her life books are characterized by rich character development, as the author skillfully weaves together the stories of diverse topics, illuminating journeys, challenges, and triumphs. Through books, the author explores themes such as love, passion, victory, identity, personal growth, and the search for meaning, offering readers profound insights and moments of introspection.

Beyond Zoë's professional accomplishments, she also has a rich and multifaceted life outside of publishing. This book is a testament to her commitment to providing valuable insights and practical guidance. The author's books are often praised for their ability to evoke empathy in readers, fostering a deep connection between the readers and the valuable insights they encounter within the pages.

The author is a distinguished authority in various fields of study, bringing a wealth of knowledge and experience to her thought-provoking non-fiction works. As you delve into Zoë's manuscripts, you can expect to embark on an intellectual journey guided by Zoë's profound insights and intentional thought-provoking passion for self -development. Her non-fiction works continue to push the boundaries of knowledge, inviting readers to expand their horizons and gain a deeper understanding of life and its impact on our success.

Zoë's works have been praised for their meticulous research, insightful analysis, and the way they challenge readers to think critically about the world around them.

Any one of Zoë's latest book,....

1. Unlocking Infinity: Master the Art of Longevity

Learn How to, Boost Your Brain Health, Recharge Your Immune System and Restore Youthful Balance in 3 Easy Steps

2. Living Your Best Life: Radiate from Within

Ultimate Guide to Finding Purpose & Fulfillment in 3 Easy Steps.

3. Redefining Aging: The Art of Living Alone

How to Find Joy in Independence, Live Fearlessly & Maintain Longevity

4. Longevity: The Art of Aging Backwards

Step-by-Step Guide to Renew, Restore and Reverse Aging Mentally, Physically & Spiritually

5. Journeying Alone, Journeying Strong: Navigating Aging Alone Without Children

Self-Help Guide to Finding Inner Strength, Peace, Joy & Fulfillment in Childless Aging

6. Mastering the Steps to Success: Achieving Success at Every Rung

Proven Strategies for Overcoming Obstacles and Reaching Greatness. Develop, Learn, Succeed

7. The Positivity Code: Supercharge Your Life with Positive Thinking

Learn The Art of Positive Thinking, Changing Your Life One Thought at a Time

8. The Growth Mindset Code: Cracking the Secrets to Success

Comprehensive Guide to Breaking Limits with A Growth Mindset, Cultivating Unlimited Possibilities

9. The Superfood Prescription: Refuel Your Mind & Body

100 Supercharged Foods to Revitalize & Transform Your Health

… is another testament to her dedication to delivering enlightening and captivating non-fiction literature. Whether you're a seasoned reader of non-fiction or new to the genre Zoë's work is sure to engage, inform, and inspire.

To stay updated on **Zoë Publishing's** latest projects and musings, visit us on **facebook.com/zoepublishing** and follow us on Instagram & Tik Tok **(@zoepublishing)**